Fundamentals for Factors

How You Can Make
Large Returns in Small Receivables

Jeff Callender

DASH POINT PUBLISHING

Federal Way, Washington

Fundamentals for Factors
How You Can Make
Large Returns in Small Receivables

by Jeff Callender

Published by:
Dash Point Publishing, Inc.
P.O. Box 25591
Federal Way, WA 98093-2591 U.S.A.

Website: www.DashPointPublishing.com

This publication is designed to provide accurate and authoritative information in regard to the subject mattered covered. It is sold with the understanding that the author and publisher are not engaged in rendering professional services. If professional advice or other expert assistance is required, the services of a competent professional person should be sought.

While every reasonable attempt has been made to obtain accurate information, the author and publisher hereby disclaim any liability for problems due to errors, omissions, or changed information in this publication.

Fictitious names of people and companies are used in this book. Any similarity between these and names of actual people and companies is unintended and purely coincidental.

Library of Congress Control Number: 2012943555
ISBN: 978-1-938837-01-2 (Paperback)
ISBN: 978-1-938837-13-5 (PDF)
ISBN: 978-1-938837-19-7 (Kindle)
ISBN: 978-1-938837-07-4 (ePub)

Printed in the United States of America.

Contents

Part 1

Factoring 101

"Now wait a minute... Why would a business owner want to sell his receivables? Most business owners probably don't even know they *can.*"

1
Introduction

In 1994 I began a home based business that uses an investment method that has been in existence for literally centuries. It is practiced widely across the USA, is even more common in Europe, and is of course completely legal yet has little government regulation.

You can do this from your home just like I do or from an outside office – and it won't take you years to begin making consistent, high yield returns. A few months is usually enough for most people – ordinary people like you and me. You can do it full-time as a business or part-time and keep your regular job.

Let me explain.

Traditional Investments

Due to the economy and very low interest rates, most people are making almost nothing in traditional investments. If your money is in CDs and money markets with rates around 1 and 2% APR (Annual Percentage Rate), you're making at best about $17 a month on a $10,000 CD investment. That's pitiful!

Maybe you're playing the stock market, trying to make a better return. Have you followed the advice of brokers and other stock or options experts – only to lose more money than you've made? Maybe a lot more?

Consider this:

- If you have investment funds making very low returns...
- And you're tired of the stock market's roller coaster ride...
- And you've had it with commissioned brokers or self-proclaimed gurus selling expensive advice that's too often wrong...
- And you're ready to try something new where YOU make hands-on decisions...
- And you're looking for consistent annualized returns in the middle to high double digits...

Let me introduce an alternative that may be new to you but has been around a very long time. Consider investing in the accounts receivable of one or a few small businesses in your area. That is, buy companies' fresh invoices. They're worth money: the customers have an obligation to pay them.

Now wait a minute... Why would a business owner want to sell his receivables? Most business owners probably don't even know they *can*.

Simple: waiting 30 or 45 days to receive payment can put a real squeeze on a company's cash flow. If they make a product or have to meet payroll, waiting that long can mean a cash shortfall when materials are needed for new orders, or when payday rolls around every week or two.

How can they meet these critical expenses if they haven't been paid what they're owed and don't have enough cash reserves to cover these critical expenses? Answer: they can sell a valuable asset – their receivables.

Cash flow problems keep many businesses from growing like they want to and could if they only had adequate cash on hand. Selling receivables at a discount is how to get this cash quickly – and get it without creating debt, which a bank loan does...IF a bank will even consider them. And just waiting to hear if a bank loan has been approved (which most aren't) can take months.

Did You Know...

Companies often discount invoices to customers on a 2 net 10 basis. That is, if a customer pays in 10 days, they can deduct 2% from the face value of the invoice.

Many businesses gladly give this discount to get paid faster. However, most customers are not equipped or inclined to take advantage of this discount. The vast majority wait 30 or more days and pay the full amount. And **therein lies your opportunity.**

If you buy invoices at rates similar to or less than what many businesses are already willing to offer their customers, look what happens:

- The business owner gets the cash up front to meet payroll, purchase materials, pay taxes, and anything else he needs.
- He's not paying more than he would with 2 net 10 terms, which he's usually willing to give anyway.
- He doesn't run the risk of customers taking the 2% discount and STILL taking 30 or more days to pay – which happens.
- He grows his business with excellent cash flow, and thus has more receivables to sell you.
- *You* get a tremendous return on investment which continues as your client grows.

Win-win all the way around!

This practice of selling receivables for less than their face value has been done for many, many years. The Romans did it. The Pilgrims did it. It's been a standard business practice in Europe for a long time, and it's widely done in the U.S. even though many people here aren't aware of it.

Buying and selling accounts receivable is called factoring. As you can see, by selling their business-to-business and business-to-government invoices to factors, companies can obtain cash quickly to run their operations and grow without a bank loan.

What about Competition?

There are many large factoring companies out there. Search the internet for factors and you'll find many, many companies listed. Most are larger factors.

However, most bigger factors don't want to buy invoices of very small companies with volumes less than $10,000 per month. Finding factors willing to accept such small companies can be a challenge for very small business owners.

Why? Big factors can't purchase such small accounts profitably – their overhead is too high. The few that say they do purchase such small accounts usually don't really want them, and *might* accept them in hopes the small client will grow into their profitability range. Most larger factors either turn away very small companies or require monthly minimum volume and discounts and require long-term contracts, if they accept very small clients at all.

That creates a **wonderful niche** for the small factor and savvy independent investor **in a very, very large market.**

Purchasing business accounts receivable can be a rewarding way of making consistent, excellent returns while helping small businesses with their cash flow needs. But you must know how to do it and risks are involved, of course.

The Purpose of
The Small Factor Series

Helping you understand factoring, how you profit, and the risks that go with the territory are what this series of books is all about.

The first book in the series, *Factoring Wisdom: A Preview of Buying Receivables*, gathers, sorts, and presents scores of factoring topics. Grouped alphabetically by subject, this volume provides a thumbnail sketch of the information, experiences, and "words to the wise" that are found throughout all my books and ebooks. They are condensed here for an easily grasped summary of factoring and its many finer points. This book includes quotes from all books in The Small Factor Series as well as many other titles, and makes both an excellent introduction and summary to these works. Thus you will benefit from reading this book prior to – and after – reading the others. If you're intrigued with this subject and curious as to just what factoring is all about, this digest is a good way to begin learning about it.

The purposes of *Fundamentals for Factors,* the second book in the series which you are now reading, are to:

- Provide introductory information about the practice of factoring small receivables.
- Present the remarkable returns you can make.
- Show how this can be done on a part-time basis if you want to keep your present job, if you're approaching retirement, or already retired.
- Show how this can be a full-time business if you desire.
- Indicate how much capital is needed.
- Provide an introduction to risks and basic risk management tools.
- Encourage you to consider your personal tolerance for risk and the tolerance for risk of those people close to you.
- Help you discern if factoring is an appropriate investment of your time and money, given your present life's circumstances.

While this book gives you the fundamentals you need to know before entering the factoring arena, it does not provide you with the "nuts and bolts" of how to actually factor receivables day-to-day: the forms needed, procedures to follow, record keeping practices, and the like. All that information and much more are provided in detail in book 3 of this series, *How to Run a Small Factoring Business.*

The fourth book of this series, *Factoring Case Studies: Essential Lessons from 30 Real Factoring Clients,* provides real-life examples of several small factors and clients they have funded...for better and for worse. The numerous case studies come from the experiences of small factors around the country and illustrate what desirable clients – as well as those who turned out not so desirable – look and act like. If a picture is worth a thousand words, these case studies are pictures (though not literal photos) of the principles and lessons in the first books, and relate some very educational – and quite interesting – personal stories. Used together, The Small Factor Series provides thorough instruction in the entire process of investing in receivables of small companies.

If after finishing this book you decide you want to be a small factor either part-time or full-time, *How to Run a Small Factoring Business* is a must read. You'll find yourself referring to it constantly as you start and continue to purchase small receivables to earn very high returns. *Factoring Case Studies* will make the forms, suggestions, and daily procedures come alive and illustrate in very human stories what you've learned in the first two works.

The last book in the series, *Marketing Methods for Small Factors & Brokers*, includes contributions from eight professionals in the industry who each describe marketing tools that have and have not worked for them. The book describes numerous marketing methods, including networking groups, cold calls, direct mail, trade shows, referrals from clients/customers/brokers/other factors, public speaking, press releases, several online techniques including social media, and many more. Most important, each writer describes his/her experience as to the value of each method they've used.

A book not included in The Small Factor Series, *Factoring: Sell Your Invoices Today & Get Cash Tomorrow*, is written for business owners who may be unfamiliar with factoring or who have some exposure to factoring but want to learn more. It will help them understand normal procedures, see how factoring can help their cash flow, and learn the difference between factoring and traditional loans or venture capital. This knowledge will make starting a factoring relationship much less intimidating.

So let's begin with *Fundamentals for Factors.* You will learn in the pages that follow "How You Can Make Large Returns in Small Receivables." Time to get started!

2
The Past, Present, and Future of Factoring

The History of Factoring

Factoring has been practiced for centuries. The ancient Phoenicians supposedly used a primitive form of factoring, and the Romans were known to sell promissory notes at a discount. The word "factor" itself comes from Latin, the language of Rome. It means "to do" or "to make." Our word "factory" comes from the same root, and everyone knows a factory is a building "where things are made." Our dictionary says "factor" in Latin means "doer" – and we might say factors are the people who are "business doers" – they make business happen.

The Pilgrims' journeys to America were financed by advances from a factor who provided the funds to pay for passage. They repaid this money with earnings in their new home which they sent back to England.

Over time as the colonies grew, a London businessman sold raw materials (timber and furs) the colonists provided to English businesses. He guaranteed the colonists' credit for buying refined goods they needed from England, and collected the colonists' payments to the London merchants. He kept a discount for his efforts, and a colonial form of factoring was established.

Down through the years factoring has continued in England and throughout Europe, where it is a common business practice today. Most Europeans are familiar with the procedure, unlike ordinary Americans who usually have never heard of it. Despite this widespread lack of awareness here, factoring is quite prevalent in the American economy and well known to large businesses, many of whom became large through factoring their receivables.

Factoring as we now know it in the U.S. began to be commonly practiced in the garment industry in New York in the early 20th Century, and has continued so to this day. Virtually all companies who manufacture clothing utilize factors and began their business doing so. It is one of the few American industries in which a factor or broker looking for business does not need to explain how it works. As one factor put it, "None of us would be wearing clothes today if it weren't for factors." Now there's something to think about.

Up until the 1980's factoring transactions were limited to rather large volume clients. However with the savings and loan problems that occurred during that decade, banks became more tightly regulated and business loans to small and medium sized businesses became harder to acquire due to the regulations and the much greater care exercised by banks. That restriction to the money supply made factoring one of the few financing alternatives for smaller businesses, and factors emerged who were willing to take on smaller businesses than those previously factored.

During the 1990's, many factors were funding receivables larger than $10,000 per month in invoice volume. Smaller factors willing to purchase very small receivables, those under $10,000, began to surface.

Factoring Now

Meanwhile factoring in the U.S. today is a multi-billion dollar industry. Medium and large factors continue to fund clients who factor hundreds of thousands to millions of dollars every year and even every month. Small factors continue to emerge, serving the huge market of small and very small businesses. These little companies are often start-ups and young firms which make up the vast majority of the number of businesses in this country.

Two alternate forms of factoring are also widely prevalent today and deserve mention, though neither is known by the term "factoring."

18

1. Merchants who accept credit card payments are in essence factoring receivables: they're accepting immediate cash for a future payment, and paying a discount for doing so.

2. Payday loan centers are doing the same thing – the person receiving cash for an upcoming paycheck is paying a discount to get immediate cash for money he has earned. However, the cost to the client for these transactions is significantly higher than regular factoring, and personally I cringe when someone says, "Factoring is like a payday loan for businesses." It's far more than that and not nearly as costly.

Both these examples have different "clients" and "customers" than business-to-business factoring transactions, but the principle of paying a discount for immediate cash is the same.

The Future of Factoring

I am sometimes asked what I think the future holds for business-to-business factoring. Will it continue to exist? Will the demand for it remain, especially among very small businesses? My answer is a definite "Yes."

As private investors see the potential returns available in factoring and are inclined to invest less in Wall Street and other traditional markets, the small factor ranks will grow. Further, the potential businesses that will benefit from factoring will be far greater in number than the very small factors ready to fund them.

Factoring is often called a "recession-proof" business. When the economy is good, businesses need cash to fuel their growth. Banks, conservative institutions that they are, will not provide all the capital needed. They view loans to startups and young companies as too risky and routinely require tax records and business financials dating back two, three, or even five years. This automatically disqualifies young businesses from bank loans. SBA loans are also hard to obtain and are quite small.

Even if a small business obtains an SBA loan, it's only a matter of time before it will need more cash if it continues to grow. The same is true for any loan for that matter: loans generate debt which must be paid back. When funds from a loan or line of credit are exhausted, more are needed. If banks will not provide new loans or higher lines, the business must find cash somewhere else.

Ultimately selling receivables not only provides the cash needed, but factoring becomes in essence an unlimited credit line. More cash is available the more invoices a company creates. Therefore in good times, companies need cash...and find it with factoring.

On the other hand, when the economy is not good banks become even more careful with their lending requirements. Capital, even for existing businesses (let alone start-ups) becomes more difficult to obtain. In tight economic times, the stock market flounders or becomes volatile, businesses announce layoffs, people are more careful with their money, and invoices are paid more slowly by customers. This kind of restricted market makes the demand for factoring – which is more concerned with the creditworthiness of customers than the clients – that much higher. Therefore in bad times, companies need cash...and find it with factoring. Factoring is a recession-proof business.

In recent years with the economic difficulties that began in 2008, bank lending virtually disappeared for small businesses. This brought factoring to light for people who had never heard of or considered it before. Thus factoring has become more mainstream and acceptable, which has increased both the number of prospective clients and the number of factors serving them.

Online exchanges for buying receivables by such as The Receivables Exchange and Receivables Market, and the ability to buy portions of invoices by a number of corporate and private buyers such as QuarterSpot, are providing more exposure (and some competition) to traditional factoring. However, like banks, those groups alone will not fill the financial needs of all the businesses needing money, and the need for factors will continue. These online services will in fact provide a new venue for factors of any size to invest their funds.

Over time all factors experience financial losses. This goes with the territory and must be accepted by everyone entering the field at any level. The key is to keep these losses small and non-catastrophic. Those who take heavy losses usually leave the business or are absorbed by other factors. Slowly increasing competition – and mere survival – will require that factors have well refined practices, exercise prudent judgment, utilize effective legal documents and counsel, and be especially vigilant against fraud and crippling losses. Those who do will survive and prosper.

As long as businesses need cash there will always be a demand for someone to provide it. That means the necessity for prudent and prosperous small factors will be with us for a long time to come.

3
Factoring Basics

Factoring Defined

Factoring is defined as the purchase of accounts receivable, or invoices, at a discount. That is, a factor buys business-to-business or business-to-government invoices at a price that is less than their face value. Factoring is not a loan with interest due, but the purchase of an asset for which a discount is paid. That distinction is important so keep it in mind.

In a nutshell, it works like this. Suppose a small factor investor purchases a $1,000 invoice. He might advance 80% of the value of that invoice and in 30 days receive payment for the full amount. When the payment arrives, he repays himself the $800 advanced, keeps the discount of 5% or $50 as income, and rebates the client the remaining 15%, or $150. Thus the client has paid $50 to receive $950, $800 of which he received immediately.

That instant cash allows him to meet a myriad of business needs: payroll, taxes, purchase supplies, receive a discount for paying with cash, accept orders he might have turned away, extend credit to a desirable customer, and much more. Factoring receivables for these common business needs is a dependable means of providing capital for a company when traditional funds are unavailable.

At this point let's clarify two terms used throughout this book. 1) The *client* is the business who has invoices the factor purchases. 2) The *customer* (or debtor) is the company who has received the product or service from the client, and will be paying the invoices. Keeping this distinction in mind let's take a brief look at two potential clients and how factoring can help them.

Two Real-Life Examples

Earl Butler owns a small company, Power Washing, Inc., which regularly washes the fleets of trucks, busses and vans of his eight customers. These include a school bus company, a small moving van business, small local transit busses, and vans of a non-profit organization. He has a handful of employees and must meet payroll every other week.

While these accounts pay regularly and he has few problems collecting his money, his customers take anywhere from three weeks to two months to pay his invoices. His monthly billing ranges between $5,000 to $8,000 per month, and his invoices typically are from $250 to $1,000 in size.

Earl is a perfect candidate for the services of a factor: he has customers who are stable, pay dependably, and he runs an honest and valuable service business. He has a history of very little bad debt, his customers are happy with his service, and he practices sound business management. However, finding a factor willing to accept his account has been difficult. Why?

Most established factors consider his company's monthly factoring volume too low to be profitable. Some require at least $10,000 per month in total volume, while others require $20,000 to $50,000 in minimum monthly volume. Larger factors' minimums usually start at $100,000 per month. If he doesn't have large enough volume, he will be unable to grow his business from factoring his receivables because the majority of factors will not accept him as a client.

+ + +

Ben Vaughn has a contract with a big-name wireless phone company to repair and upgrade wireless phones in his town. Ben's is a part-time business, and his invoices typically add up to about $500 per week, all with this one big customer. While individual bills for his work are frequently no more than $50 to $100, he can group them to add up to a single invoice of about $1,000 every couple weeks. Because they all go to the same customer, grouping bills this way is preferable for both Ben and the phone company.

24

However, Ben's customer takes longer to pay than he can afford. Waiting 30 to 60 days is the norm, and Ben has trouble keeping enough parts in stock to make the repairs. This doesn't matter to the large customer, but it makes running his business next to impossible without some way of converting his receivables into ready cash.

Factoring is a logical move for Ben. If he were to sell his invoices to a factor and receive a 70% to 80% advance on their value, he would easily be able to keep all his needed supplies in stock and could even expand his business if he chooses. But like Earl, Ben has had trouble finding a factor interested in accepting his $2,000 monthly invoice volume. His account is too small for a regular factor to service profitability. If he could find a factor who, like himself, were a small business person—perhaps one providing factoring services part-time or on a limited basis—he would be able to solve his cash flow problem.

These two real-life examples show the dilemma confronting millions of small business owners. Their viable business could prosper and flourish with adequate capital. Yet they are unable to obtain money from traditional lending sources like banks, usually due to being in business for too little time, a blemish on their credit history, or some other common reason. Moreover, they can't even persuade non-traditional capital sources like factors to accept them.

This dilemma exposes two stark facts: there exist 1) a gaping hole for financing very small business, and 2) an enormous niche for a unique breed of entrepreneur: the small factor.

The Need for Small Factors

In 1994 I entered the world of factoring with no business background at all. Beginning as a broker (one who places business owners in need of factoring with well-matched funding sources), the need for small factors quickly became apparent. As a broker, I was competing for the larger, more desirable accounts. Yet in the process of marketing and beating the bushes for business, I found many more small companies than larger companies in need of

25

factoring. What's more, in those days there were virtually no factors willing to accept very small accounts like those of Earl and Ben.

The reason was – and remains – simple: a factor's overhead expenses (staff, office rent, cost of capital, and monthly expenses running the business) demand a certain level of income to break even. Small accounts generally take as much (and often more) maintenance as larger accounts. The cost for larger factors to service these small accounts is simply more than the income the accounts generate.

However, it stands to reason that if a small factor with very little overhead can service accounts of small businesses and provide value to his clients, a reasonable profit and viable business can be realized.

It didn't take long to discover that factoring small receivables would generate more income than I could earn from the commissions made brokering larger accounts. How is this so? First, there are many small companies out there who can benefit from factoring, and they're not that hard to find. Second, making more income as a small factor than as a broker is a matter of simple arithmetic.

Factoring brokers typically earn a commission of 10% to 15% of the factor's discount. If a factor earns 5% from $20,000 worth of invoices, the factor earns $1,000. A 10% broker commission of this $1,000 factoring discount is $100, while a 15% broker commission is $150. Thus a broker will earn $100 to $150 from $20,000 worth of brokered invoices if the factor is making a discount of 5%.

However, if this same broker comes across a client with only $5,000 worth of invoices — a client the same larger factor would probably reject — and the broker-turned-small factor makes 5% in factoring discounts from the $5,000, he earns $250. In other words, he makes $100 to $150 *more* than he does from brokering invoices *four times as large.*

With this simple math and an understanding of the number of businesses in need of this service, my career as a small factor was born. That was 1994. The same numbers still work today.

Part 2

Factoring
and You

"People frequently ask me, 'How much money can I make as a small factor?' The answer depends...."

4

Return on
Your Investment

How Much You Can Make

People frequently ask me, "How much money can I make as a small factor?" The answer depends on how much money you have to invest – your own or someone else's – and whether you wish to make factoring a full-time business or part time investment. Either works quite well.

The returns you can make are essentially the same, in terms of annual percentage rate (APR) realized. The return depends on three things:

1. Percentage advanced.
2. Discount charged.
3. Length of time until the invoice is paid.

If you have brokered factoring deals or just considered doing so, have you ever wondered what return factors of larger receivables make? Let's see what their returns might be.

Because there are no regulations or mandated factoring discounts, factors can charge whatever the market will bear. Discounts can be calculated in a myriad of ways, but generally there is a base discount (x % for the first x days) and an incremental discount (x % for x days following the base period). Many larger factors require application or due diligence fees, as well as other charges for additional services such as billing if they provide it.

Discounts for clients factoring over $10,000 or $20,000 monthly vary widely; the following rates are normal advances and discounts for larger factors:

Factor 1
Advance: 80%
Discount: 3% first 30 days
+1% per 10 days thereafter

Factor 1's discounts break down like this:

# Days	Discount
0-30	3%
31-40	4%
41-50	5%
51-60	6%
61-70	7%
71-80	8%
81-90	9%

Factor 2
Advance: 85%
Discount: 2% first 15 days
+1.5% each 15 days thereafter

Factor 2's discounts break down this way:

# Days	Discount
0-15	2.0%
16-30	3.5%
31-45	5.0%
46-60	6.5%
61-75	8.0%
76-90	9.5%

How to Calculate Returns

How do we calculate the return these factors are making? To calculate the annual return based on the full amount of the invoice, the formula is:

Annual return = Discount % x 365 / # of days to earn discount

In the case of Factor 1, this formula for receivables that pay in 30 days is:

Annual return = 3% Discount for 30 days x 365 / 30, or
Annual return = 3% x 365 / 30 = **36.5%**

So for every $100,000 worth of invoices Factor 1 purchases that pay in 30 days, he's making 3% or $3,000. Over a year that's a 36.5% annual return, every single month, as long as the invoices are factored and paid in that time frame. Not bad.

But wait – we've overlooked something. The above formula assumes a 100% advance. In order to limit their risk and assure their discount, *factors don't give 100% advances!* Factor 1, in fact, gives an 80% advance, which is pretty standard. That means the monthly percentage of the returns actually earned is higher than the 3% of the invoice amount, and the APR is higher than the 36.5% annual return. How much higher?

The way we calculated the monthly return of 3% is to take the monthly discount income and divide it by the invoice amount:

Discount / **Invoice** = Monthly Return on **Invoice** Amt
$3,000 / $100,000 = 3.0%

So dividing the monthly discount income by the **advance** amount shows the actual percentage earned, which is now higher because it is based on the **advance** amount ($80,000) instead of the **invoice** amount ($100,000):

Discount / **Advance** = Monthly Return on **Advance** Amt
$3,000 / $80,000 = 3.75%

Multiply the Monthly Return percent by 365 and divide by the number of days to earn the discount (for an annual return) and you get

3.75% x 365 / 30 = APR
3.75% x 365 / 30= **45.625% APR**

So with the discounts Factor 1 is charging, when invoices pay in 30 days he is making 45.625% APR.

To summarize, we make four quick calculations to arrive at the APR:
1. Advance = Invoice Amount x Advance %
2. Discount = Invoice Amount x Discount %
3. Return % = Discount / Advance
4. APR = Return % x 365 / # of days to earn discount

Let's use this "calculator box" to see **Factor 2's** return.

1. Advance: $100,000 x 85%   = $85,000
2. Discount for 30 Days 3.5%   = $3,500
3. 30 Day Return %: $3,500 / $85,000   = 4.1177%
4. APR: 4.1177% x 365 / 30 = **50.00987% APR**

So Factor 2 at the 30 day mark is making an annualized return of 50%.

These are certainly healthy returns! But not all invoices pay in 30 days. What if their invoices take 60 days to pay instead of 30?

Factor 1
1. Advance: $100,000 x 80%   = $80,000
2. Discount for 60 Days 6%   = $6,000
3. 60 Day Return %: $6,000 / $80,000 = 7.5%
4. APR: 7.5% x 365 / 60   = **45.625% APR**

Thus Factor 1 is making the same return at 60 days that he is at 30 days because his discount is incrementing the same amount every 30 days (3%).

What about **Factor 2** at 60 days?

1. Advance: $100,000 x 85%   = $85,000 advance
2. Discount for 60 days: $100,000 x 6.5%   = $6,500
3. 60 Day Return %: $6,500 / $85,000   = 7.6471%
4. APR: 7.6471% x 365 / 60 = **46.52%** APR

Here we see Factor 2's return diminishes over time (50% at 30 days to 46.52% at 60 days) because the factoring discounts are more for the first 30 days than they are for the second 30 days.

34

While these formulas are not complex, for those who are "mathematically challenged" – or who just don't want to go through these four steps – an inexpensive calculator is available which performs the above formula instantly. In an Excel spreadsheet, you can immediately calculate the APR for any transaction of any size. You can obtain the calculator from <u>Dash Point Publishing.</u>

Returns for Small Receivables

Small clients take larger factors approximately the same staff time to service as larger clients take, yet bring in smaller discounts due to lower volume. Therefore larger factors often charge smaller clients higher discounts – if they even accept these smaller clients in the first place.

Lower demand and higher discounts for very small clients create a perfect niche for small investors who, compared to large factors, maintain very low overhead. How do small factor investors keep expenses far lower than large factors?

1. **By having no or few employees**: payroll and employee taxes and benefits are a major expense of large factors. With a relatively small client load, account managers and other support staff are not needed.
2. **By working from home or a small office**, rather than a large office in expensive business parks or complexes, rent expenses are slim to none.
3. **By keeping operating costs (telephone, utilities, travel, etc.) to a minimum**, these are also very small outlays compared to what large factors pay.

Calculating Your Returns

Calculating your returns as a small factor is done exactly as already described, and depends on the same three variables:

1. Percentage advanced.
2. Discount charged.
3. Length of time until the invoice is paid.

The first two are completely up to you, insofar as they are acceptable to your factoring client. You have less control over number 3; however, with some simple due diligence you can get a fairly good idea of what to expect from most paying business customers. You can refuse to factor those with no credit, poor credit, or who have a history of taking longer to pay than you want to wait.

The APR Calculator mentioned earlier works exactly the same for determining small factors' returns as it does for those of large factors. However for those who want to see the rationale behind the returns of small factors, the following will be helpful.

To calculate your return, let's assume you give an 80% advance and charge 5% for the first 30 days and 1% additional for each 10 days thereafter. This is a competitive advance and discount structure for clients factoring less than $10,000 per month. Some charge less, many charge more.

Small Factor
Advance: 80%
Discount: 5% first 30 days
+1% each 10 days thereafter
Your discounts break down this way:

# Days	Discount
0-30	5%
31-40	6%
41-50	7%
51-60	8%
61-70	9%
71-80	10%
81-90	11%

Let's calculate what your return would be on an invoice that pays in 30 days. But instead of $100,000 worth of invoices, let's use the realistic figure of $1,000.

1. Advance: $1,000 x 80% = $800
2. Discount for 30 days: $1,000 x 5% = $50
3. 30 Day Return %: $50 / $800 = 6.25%
4. APR: 6.25% x 365 / 30 = **76.04%** APR

What is your return if an invoice pays in 60 days?

1. Advance: $1,000 x 80% = $800
2. Discount for 60 days: $1,000 x 8% = $80 discount
3. 60 Day Return %: $80 / $800 = 10%
4. APR: 10% x 365 / 60 = **60.08%** APR

Like Factor 2, your return decreases in time because your discount is higher for the first 30 days than it is for the second 30 days. To keep your discounts consistent over time, structure your rates so that each 30 day increment is the same as your first 30 day discount, as Factor 1 does. That is, you could charge

- 5% for each 30 days, or
- 5% for the first 30 days plus 2.5% every 15 days thereafter, or
- 5% for the first 30 days plus 1.67% every 10 days thereafter, or
- 2.5% every 15 days, or
- 1.67% every 10 days.

Any of these combinations will provide a 76% APR return at 30, 60 and 90 days.

Now back to the question, "How much money can I make as a small factor?" To answer, let's look at charts that assume we're charging a 5% discount for 30 days (no matter what combination above is used to get there), and that invoices pay in 30 days. How much would you make at these rates? The answer depends on the volume you factor, as Chart 1 shows.

Charts of Returns

Chart 1
0% Cost of Capital, 80% Advance

Amt of Invcs	80% Adv	5% Avg Discount	0% Cost of Money	Income Before Overhd	APR w/ 80% adv
10,000	8,000	500	0	500	76.04%
25,000	20,000	1,250	0	1,250	76.04%
50,000	40,000	2,500	0	2,500	76.04%
100,000	80,000	5,000	0	5,000	76.04%
250,000	200,000	12,500	0	12,500	76.04%
500,000	400,000	25,000	0	25,000	76.04%

As you can see, you continue to make the same APR regardless of the volume you are factoring. However, the amount of money you actually make depends on the volume of invoices you buy.

If you buy $10,000 worth of invoices, you advance $8,000 and make $500 in discounts. If you buy $50,000 worth of invoices you need $40,000 for advances and make $2,500 in discounts. These are very attainable figures for people with this amount of money to invest, and represent realistic monthly amounts for people who invest in small receivables on a part-time basis.

Those with more funds can make enough in discounts to earn a full-time living. With $80,000 to advance toward $100,000 worth of invoices, discounts are $5,000; $200,000 in advances will produce discounts of $12,500, and so on. This is a very comfortable income for many people.

Now, suppose instead of advancing 80% you advance less – say 70%. How will this affect your discounts and your returns?

Chart 2
0% Cost of Capital, 70% Advance

Amt of Invcs	70% Adv	5% Avg Discount	0% Cost of Money	Before Overhd	APR w/ 70% adv
10,000	7,000	500	0	500	86.90%
25,000	17,500	1,250	0	1,250	86.90%
50,000	35,000	2,500	0	2,500	86.90%
100,000	70,000	5,000	0	5,000	86.90%
250,000	175,000	12,500	0	12,500	86.90%
500,000	350,000	25,000	0	25,000	86.90%

With lower advances you continue to make the same discounts because your discount rates have remained at 5%. However you need less capital because your advances are lower and therefore your returns are higher. As you can see, with a 70% advance and the same 5% discounts at 30 days, your APR has jumped to 86.90%.

Now let's suppose you are going to use other people's money to purchase invoices. Why? Perhaps you have very little of your own money to invest, or you've invested as much of your own capital as you intend. Another possibility is friends or relatives have seen your success and are interested in investing with you. Finally, perhaps you simply have more clients requesting your service than you have available funds, and now you need to secure outside capital. Any of these circumstances are quite possible.

You need to pay something for this extra working capital. Let's suppose you secure funds at a 12% APR rate; that is, you pay monthly interest of 1%. What will your income and APR become using these borrowed funds? Charts 3 and 4 show them using 80% and 70% advances, respectively.

Chart 3
12% APR Cost of Capital, 80% Advance

Amt of Invcs	80% Adv	5% Avg Discount	1% Mo. Cost of Money	Income Before Overhd	APR w/ 80% adv
10,000	8,000	500	80	420	63.88%
25,000	20,000	1,250	200	1,050	63.88%
50,000	40,000	2,500	400	2,100	63.88%
100,000	80,000	5,000	800	4,200	63.88%
250,000	200,000	12,500	2,000	10,500	63.88%
500,000	400,000	25,000	4,000	21,000	63.88%

Chart 4
12% APR Cost of Capital, 70% Advance

Amt of Invcs	70% Adv	5% Avg Discount	1% Mo. Cost of Money	Income Before Overhd	APR w/ 70% adv
10,000	7,000	500	70	430	74.74%
25,000	17,500	1,250	175	1,075	74.74%
50,000	35,000	2,500	350	2,150	74.74%
100,000	70,000	5,000	700	4,300	74.74%
250,000	175,000	12,500	1,750	10,750	74.74%
500,000	350,000	25,000	3,500	21,500	74.74%

Now suppose you need to pay a bit more for your capital, perhaps 18% APR, or 1.5% per month. Charts 5 and 6 provide the income and APR.

Chart 5
18% Cost of Capital, 80% Advance

Amt of Invcs	80% Adv	5% Avg Discount	1.5% Mo. Cost of Money	Income Before Overhd	APR w/ 80% adv
10,000	8,000	500	120	380	57.79%
25,000	20,000	1,250	300	950	57.79%
50,000	40,000	2,500	600	1,900	57.79%
100,000	80,000	5,000	1,200	3,800	57.79%
250,000	200,000	12,500	3,000	9,500	57.79%
500,000	400,000	25,000	6,000	19,000	57.79%

Chart 6
18% Cost of Capital, 70% Advance

Amt of Invcs	70% Adv	5% Avg Discount	1.5% Mo. Cost of Money	Income Before Overhd	APR w/ 70% adv
10,000	7,000	500	105	395	68.65%
25,000	17,500	1,250	263	988	68.65%
50,000	35,000	2,500	525	1,975	68.65%
100,000	70,000	5,000	1,050	3,950	68.65%
250,000	175,000	12,500	2,625	9,875	68.65%
500,000	350,000	25,000	5,250	19,750	68.65%

Obviously the less you pay for your capital and the less you advance, the higher your income and returns. Because you set the discounts and advances insofar as your clients agree to them, you have a fair degree of control over the income and returns you make, the volume of invoices you buy, the amount of factoring funds you have to invest, and the time you want to spend as a small factor.

As you can see, you can make remarkable returns as a small factor even when borrowing at a fairly high rate. These returns are fairly predictable once you learn your clients' factoring needs and habits. In many cases clients will factor on a regular basis, often weekly; this makes the returns you can make quite constant, even routine. How many other investments do you know where you can make such returns (57%, 63%, 68%, 76%, and more, as we've seen) on such a consistent and even predictable basis? Furthermore, in how many investments do you, the investor, have such control not only over your return, but in the daily management of how the money is actually made? While factoring is not a passive investment, you have tremendous control over your money. Only bad debt losses will lower these returns, and as we'll see there are strategies and tools to minimize the risk of such losses. Just be sure you use them!

You're probably beginning to see why purchasing the receivables of small businesses is such an attractive financial investment.

If you would like to calculate a mix of possible advances, discounts, and payment times not covered in the above charts, another calculator spreadsheet instantly computes your potential income monthly, yearly, and over five years. This calculator is provided in the same Excel file as the APR calculator mentioned earlier from Dash Point Publishing.

So far we've looked at your financial investment and returns. What about your investment of **time**? How much time does investing in small receivables take, and how much time do you have for it? Let's look at that and some other practical matters next.

5
Practical Matters: Office, Time, and Capital

Your Office Location

One of the greatest aspects of investing in small business receivables is the flexibility of not only **when** you can do it, but **where.**

Factoring small clients either full-time or part-time is perfectly suited to a home office. Since there is little reason to use an outside facility, you have neither the extra expense of rent, nor the time, cost and inconvenience of a commute. Handled properly with the advice of your accountant, your home office can qualify as a tax deduction.

In general it's a good idea to have a specific spot set aside for your work. A spare room is ideal, but a corner of a quiet spot with a desk and basic equipment is enough to get started. With the common office machines many homes already possess – a computer with an internet connection, a telephone, and a printer/fax/ copier/scanner – you probably already have all the equipment and furniture you'll need. If you lack these, obtaining them is neither difficult nor likely to break the bank.

For those who prefer to work outside their home, a simple office works just fine. You need not rent space in an expensive business park or corporate high rise; just a basic office in a convenient location is enough to start. Beginning your operation from a one-room location is quite adequate, and will provide the distance from the distractions of home you might wish to avoid without adding high expense. You can certainly run your business today with a laptop, even an iPad or other tablet, smart phone and efax, and with these tools you can run your business from virtually anywhere you can access the internet.

Remember, one of the keys to success is keeping your overhead as low as possible. Your high returns will diminish quickly if you spend money on things you really don't need.

How Much Time Is Needed?

Sometimes people ask how much time I spend at the business. By choice I factor receivables on a part-time basis from an office in my home. Some of my clients are relatively inactive and might only factor an invoice every month or two. With the software I use and the fact that they have been my clients for some time, these accounts literally only take minutes to process both advance requests and payments when they're received.

More active clients obviously require more time. For those who factor regularly and submit several invoices each week or more, receiving payments is a regular occurrence nearly every day. Once your operation is up and running, managing these accounts might take a few hours per client each week. Not surprisingly, the most time is required when you're just starting out, learning everything, and don't have a system established yet.

How much of your time will factoring actually require? It's really impossible to say for several reasons. The following points determine the time your operation will demand:

- The number of clients you have.
- The unique needs of each client (some will require extra time while others will require very little effort once under way).
- How organized you are.
- The ease of your set-up procedures for new clients (and for you).

44

- How long you've been factoring.
- The software you use.
- How much time you choose to spend marketing.

Once your first client is under way and invoices are "in the pipeline" managing the account is relatively simple. You will receive invoices from your client to factor, determine that the invoices are good, and provide the advance. You then simply wait to receive payment and keep an eye on the time it takes to come in, notifying the client or their customer if a payment is overdue. Once payment is received, you deposit the funds, determine the rebate due, pay the rebate – and then repeat the process. While there are finer points to the operation, in a nutshell this is what you'll be doing.

You can see how factoring provides you, the investor, remarkable flexibility. You take on as many clients as you choose and funds allow, determine which client industries and customers you want to accept, make payments and deposits according to your personal schedule and clients' needs, and never once punch a clock or answer a boss's demands. You need to provide excellent service and value to your clients, but you are the boss. It is a very hands-on investment in that you are physically handling the invoices, advances, and deposits. You also determine the accounts you will accept and decline. In short, you're making all the decisions.

Part-Time

With your home or simple outside office as your base, factoring is an excellent means of making part-time or extra income. Those who choose to factor part-time might fit any of the following descriptions. They can be people who:

- Are happy with their current job and just want to make some extra money on the side.
- Are retired or are soon to retire.
- Have full-time family obligations.
- Enjoy investing as a hobby.

45

- Wish to move gradually from working for someone else to working for themselves.
- Have worked for some time in a specific industry or profession and are ready for a change or new challenge, and want to begin gradually.
- Own a business and want to add another income stream.
- Are factoring brokers who wish to expand their client base or add a profit center.
- Wish to factor full-time in the future, but lack adequate capital and/or experience to feel ready to make it a full-time business.
- Simply need to make additional income for any reason.

Factoring can be done part-time if you have as few as one or two clients, or even as many as a dozen. Some clients will require more time than others depending on the number of invoices they factor, the services you provide, the industry or nature of their work, and their billing practices.

As you would expect, when you start out the time you spend setting up a new account, performing due diligence, and exchanging paperwork and funds will take longer than it will after you've been doing it a while. Once you have some experience each transaction will become a little easier and your whole operation will gradually develop into a smooth system you won't even have to think about.

Capital Needed for Part-Time Factoring

New small factors can begin with as little as $25,000 available for client advances. If you start with just one client who is a one-person business and perhaps even part-time at that, factoring $1,000 to $3,000 per month is quite possible. These can be excellent clients as you begin, and may not demand that you have more than $5,000 to $10,000 with which to fund them.

I strongly suggest that you not use funds which are vital to your daily living expenses. In other words, don't put money you need for groceries and rent or mortgage payments into clients' advances. Your factoring funds must be discretionary investment dollars because, as with any investment, you are putting them at risk. If the funds are lost due to bad debt you won't be able to meet these basic necessities. Remember, all factors experience losses sooner or later. If your loss comes early and the lost funds should have paid the next month's mortgage payment, you have a serious problem.

However, a large number of "ordinary folks" do have adequate discretionary funds with which to begin factoring. If you stay with just one or two very small clients, you won't need much more. This dispels the common assumption that you need to be independently wealthy, receive an inheritance, or sell highly valuable assets to have enough cash to be a small factor.

How do you know how much you need? A good rule of thumb is to maintain a pool of at least 200 to 300% of anticipated cash needs per client. That is, if a client steadily factors $5,000 per month, you should have $10,000 to $15,000 set aside for this client. If you do, you should have adequate funds to meet their factoring needs. If they outgrow your funds available, you'll need to obtain more money or broker them to another factor and receive an ongoing broker's commission. Either way you continue to have income.

Why do you need more funds than a client uses each month? This cushion is needed for two reasons. First, customers do not usually pay in precise 30 day cycles. Some will pay in 15 or 20 days, others will routinely take 45 to 60 days. Thus you will have some clients whose customer payments are not received until two or even three advances have been made. This delay is, after all, the reason they're factoring in the first place. If they received all their payments immediately, your factoring services wouldn't be needed.

Second, by its very nature factoring enables clients' businesses to grow. With factoring they quickly have adequate cash flow and can take on new customers and increase sales. That means that clients who start factoring $3,000 may very likely increase their factoring volume in the coming months. As they grow, you will need more funds to fuel their growth.

Software for Part-Time Factoring

One of the biggest time savers is factoring software that meets your needs. If you are "technologically challenged" and absolutely will not use a computer, you can keep a basic business journal and track your transactions on paper. However the time you spend learning to use a computer will be made up many times over with the time the computer will save you in calculations and tracking account activity.

If you start with just one or two clients, using spreadsheets to track invoices and payments is usually adequate. You will need to know how to make basic entries, format text, link cells, and create and maintain simple formulas. If you don't know how to do this, someone familiar with these spreadsheet activities can teach you without much difficulty. Some libraries teach this class for a small fee. You don't need to know advanced functions of spreadsheets – just how to perform these basic tasks, especially calculations involving addition and percentages. You can create the spreadsheets yourself and samples are shown in *Factoring Small Receivables,* book 2 of this series.

If your part-time factoring extends to a half dozen clients or so, you may find yourself outgrowing spreadsheets and want to graduate to a database program written specifically for factoring. Having software that can provide clients with online reports will save you and them a great deal of time tracking their account. If you have created data bases and have the time and inclination to write your program, you can save money this way over the vertical market software that's for sale. If you have never created a data base before, this is not the place to start.

As your factoring business matures, your software needs can become rather involved. Your factoring investment or business will be heavily dependent on your software, so use good judgment as you consider your software alternatives.

Various commercial data base programs are written specifically for factors, and the cost of some suggest you are fairly serious about factoring as a business. The program best suited for small factors has been designed with extensive input from the author and is a web-based solution called FactorFox. To learn more about this software and view free online demos, visit www.FactorFox.com.

Full-Time

In addition to the amount of time you wish to give factoring, the other determining issue in working part-time or full-time is the amount of funds you have and the amount of income you need to generate. As we saw in the chapter, "Return on Your Investment," having less than $75,000 for advances will probably not generate enough income to make this your full-time work, unless your living expenses are quite low.

However, I strongly recommend that newcomers start very gradually, even if they have enough funds to invest to make a full-time income. While the concept behind factoring is quite simple, there are many fine points to learn and making a mistake may result in a financial loss. You are far wiser to begin investing on a very small scale and make those mistakes on a very small scale. Big mistakes can be extremely costly. So even for those who intend to factor full-time, starting part-time is a very wise move.

Investing funds in excess of $75,000 per month can provide income adequate for most people to factor as a full-time occupation. Those who choose to factor full-time might fit any of the following descriptions. They can be people who:

- Have been factoring part-time and are ready to make it their full-time work.
- Have worked for a larger factoring company, understand the business, and wish to strike out on their own.
- Have worked in an industry or business that parallels or utilizes factoring, have some exposure to it, and who are ready to work in factoring full-time.
- Have worked for some time in a specific industry or profession and are ready for a change or new challenge.

49

- Have adequate capital to use for client advances to earn enough from discounts to make full-time income, yet who are patient and prudent in their business dealings and will start slowly without putting large sums at risk too quickly.
- Have the capital to invest in professional factoring software.

Factoring on a full-time basis is an enjoyable and rewarding line of work. Just as it provides great flexibility when done part-time, working as a full-time factor is equally flexible. You determine your own hours, the location from which you work (your home or small outside office still work just fine unless you decide to take on several employees), and you still determine the clients and customers. Equipment needs remain the same as what you've used part-time.

Software for Full-Time Factoring

Factoring full-time will demand that you have very capable data base software. While you may have started with spreadsheets, you will now need a data base to adequately track your accounts. You'll soon find spreadsheets to be inadequate and an enormous time and energy drain for a full-time operation. Run your professional factoring business with professional-grade software. Quite literally, your business will depend on it.

If you have begun using FactorFox, you will no doubt continue with it as you go full-time. This is the only product available that includes, at no extra cost, direct web input of invoices and access to reports by clients, one of its many advantages. The other programs that provide this valuable feature (not all do) charge an additional price for this convenience to both the client and factor.

As you can see, to step into factoring on a full-time basis you need to take the business seriously, not only from your commitment of time but your availability of funds. This is why I so strongly recommend starting part-time and on a limited basis. Not only will it safeguard you from putting large sums on the line, but you can keep your costs much lower while you determine that factoring full-time is really what you want to do with your working hours and larger investment of dollars.

+ + +

Many people will find factoring on a part-time basis suits their lifestyle just fine. Remember, the Annual Percentage Rate you earn is high regardless of the volume you factor. The volume determines the total income you make – not your rate of return.

Whether you invest in small receivables on a part-time or full-time basis, you are providing a very needed and crucial service for your clients. In virtually all cases, the funds you make available are 1) the life blood that keeps a client's business alive, and/or 2) relieve the business owner of numerous concerns and stress. Most business owners' cash flow worries disappear when you provide advances, rebates, and receivables management in a timely and professional manner.

Your work becomes an integral and even indispensable aspect of your client's operation. You are an important business partner and will be recognized as such. What's more, while your factoring service provides quite handsome returns for you, it enables your clients to grow their businesses and increase their income as well. It is a true win-win relationship.

6
Identifying and Locating Prospective Clients

As a small factor you want clients with invoices for products or services which:

a) have been delivered

b) have no offsets against them (i.e. the client doesn't owe the customer money which will be deducted from the customer's payment), and

c) will be paid in a reasonable amount of time to your address.

The most desirable span from invoice date to payment date is between two weeks and two months in most cases.

How do you know which industries and companies have invoices like this they'll want to sell, and where do you find them? Because factoring can benefit such a broad range of businesses, it helps to establish some basic criteria as to which industries are factor-friendly.

Look for small businesses which provide products or perform services to other businesses or government and are not paid immediately. Especially if they're fairly new, the chances they will need improved cash flow – the product and service you provide – are pretty good. Service industries such as janitorial and carpet cleaning companies, guard services, temp agencies, and the like are often prized factoring clients. Skilled individuals and consultants working as independent contractors for large corporations can also be good potential clients. Product-based industries such as small manufacturing companies are also factoring prospects.

A great way to determine good potential factoring clients is to first identify desirable customers, then discover who their vendors are. In other words, what businesses have financially sound customers who take 30 or 45 days to pay? Companies who provide products or services for government agencies (schools, cities, counties, state and federal agencies), utility companies, very large corporations, and the like make excellent prospective clients. Why? They wait too long to get paid to have good cash flow (creating their need to factor) and their customers are not likely to go out of business (little risk of nonpayment for you).

To give you an idea how vast your potential client list is, I've taken just the first page from the 22-page index in my local phone book's Yellow Pages and included industries which very likely will have companies who would either

a) directly benefit from factoring their receivables (prospective clients), or
b) might be customers of potential clients (and be paying the invoices you buy), or
c) could provide good leads (referral sources).

Remember this list is only the index's first page and shows industries, not individual companies. From its sheer length you can begin to see how much potential business there is waiting for you. Some of these listings will hopefully make you think of related industries or companies in which you have experience or contacts which could lead to potential clients.

As you review this very brief list, ask yourself, "Who has business-to-business or business-to-government invoices that aren't paid immediately – or who knows companies that do?" Many of these companies will not even know about factoring.

Page 1 of Yellow Pages Index

Academies - See:
  Horse Rentals & Riding
  Schools - Academic -
    Colleges & Universities
    Secondary & Elementary
    Special Education
Accident Prevention - See:
  Safety Consultants
Accountants
Accounting & Bookkeep'g Forms - See:
  Business Forms & Systems
  Office Supplies
Acetylene Products & Services
Acoustical material
Adding Machines
Addressing & Letter Services
Adhesives & Glue
Advertising Agencies
Advertising Consultants
Advertising Specialties
Advertising - Brochures
  Advertising - Direct Mail
  Artists - Commercial
  Desktop Publishing
  Graphic Designers
  Printers
Advertising - Calendars
Advertising - Signs
Aerial Lifts
Aerial Surveys
Afro-American Goods
Agricultural Chemicals
Agricultural Equipment & Supplies
  Farm Equipment & Supplies
  Discountd - Wholesale & Mfrs
  Fertilizers - Dealers
  Irrigation Systems & Equipment
  Tractor Dealers
Aikido Instruction
Air Ambulance
Air Brakes
Air Cleaning & Purifying Equipment
Air Compressors

Air Quality - See:
  Air Pollution Control
Air Taxi & Charter Service
Air Tools
  See Tools - Pneumatic
Aircraft Avionics - Sales & Service
Aircraft Charter, Rental, & Leasing

Aircraft Hangars - See:
  Bldgs. - Metal
  Bldgs. - Pre-Cut, Prefab & Modular
Aircraft Radios & Servicing
Aircraft Schools
Aircraft Service & Maintenance
Airline Companies
Airline Ticket Agencies
Airplanes - See:
  Aircraft Charter, Rental & Leasing Svcs.
  Aircraft Dealers
  Aircraft Equipment, Parts & Supplies
  Airline Companies
Airport Parking
Airport Security - See:
  Investigators
  Security Control Equipment & Systems
  Security Guard & Patrol Services
Airport Transportation Service
Airports
Alarm Systems
  Automobile Alarms & Security Systems
  Burglar Alarms Systems & Monitoring
  Fire Alarm Systems
  Medical Alarms
  Security Control Equipment & Systems
  Sprinklers - Automatic - Fire
  Video Equipment - Security & Indust'l Sys.
Alcohol Detection & Testing
  Drug Detection Testing
Alfalfa & Alfalfa Products - See
  Discountd Dealers
All-Terrain Vehicles
Allergy Control & Filtering Equipment
Alloy Castings

Air Conditioning	Alterations - Clothing & Draperies
Air Deflectors	Alternative Fuels - See:
Truck Equipment & Parts - New	Energy Mgmt & Conservatn. Consultants
Truck Equipment & Parts - Used	Alternators & Generators - See
Van Conversions & Accessories	Automotive & Automotive Repairing
Air Duct Cleaning	Aluminum Anodizing
Air Filters	Aluminum Castings
Air Fresheners	Aluminum Hard Coating
	Ambulance Service

Identifying Prospects

Let's examine a few entries from this brief list to see how they might lead to new business. Which entries might be good clients, which could be good customers of clients, and which are potential sources of referrals?

Clients

Good clients are those who have business-to-business and/or business-to-government invoices, and who wait approximately two weeks to two months to receive payment. Review each entry and ask yourself, "Which listings have invoices like this to business or government customers?"

Under "Airport Security" we see "Security Control Equipment & Systems" and "Security Guard & Patrol Services." The "Equipment & Systems" companies would probably be manufacturers, wholesalers, and/or distributors of such equipment. They would be selling, either directly or through distribution channels, to airports, airlines, ports of entry, and any government agency or private corporation using security equipment. Consumer invoices are unlikely here. If they are not paid immediately or with credit cards and are attempting to grow or are fairly new, there are probably good prospective clients in this category.

Also in this group is "Security Guard & Patrol Services." Think about who their customers would be, under what terms they might be paid (net 30, 45, etc.), and if those payments provide adequate cash flow. As with most companies which must meet a regular payroll but wait to be paid, having enough cash to meet payroll and regular expenses can be a constant struggle. If

"Security Guard & Patrol Services" must pay their employees weekly or every other week, but are only paid monthly (which is common with security guard companies and temp agencies), there are firms in this category which will benefit from factoring.

"Drug Detection & Testing" is listed under "Alcohol Detection & Testing." These companies likely sell blood alcohol content and drug screening devices. Who buys these products? Police departments, treatment centers, hospitals, manufacturing and other safety-conscious companies who test employees for drug use, and the like: in other words, government and (probably large) corporate customers.

The "Air Deflectors" category includes "Truck Equipment & Parts" and "Van Conversions and Accessories." These firms sell to trucking companies and independent truckers. These are not transportation receivables (see "Trucking Receivables" in the chapter, "Receivables to Avoid") in that the parties are not hauling products from point A to B with meticulous paperwork needing proper signatures. They are selling equipment that many businesses – truckers – need, and they probably use ordinary invoices. If the trucking company customers are creditworthy, there are no doubt good prospects in this category.

There are other industries listed here who will have good potential factoring clients. Can you identify them? To help recognize them, ask yourself these questions:

- To whom do they sell?
- How long do they wait for payment?
- Will they benefit from immediate cash advances?

Customers

Looking over this list, who do you think would make good customers of prospective clients? We want to identify categories which will include creditworthy businesses that will probably require 30 day terms, and/or government agencies. Once these are identified, we'll want to determine who their vendors (our prospective clients) are.

Are government agencies or very large corporations listed here? Under "Academies," we see "Schools & Universities," "Secondary & Elementary," and "Special Education." This group is usually a slam dunk as acceptable customers. Public schools and universities use government Purchase Orders which means guaranteed payment. Private schools with good credit, like public schools, often have large vendor lists, and each vendor on those lists usually must wait to be paid. All you need to do is check the private schools' credit.

As far as large corporations, Airline Companies are included. With the travel industry less stable than it was prior to 9/11, this category probably is not as good as it once was. However, consider the airline industry as a whole. Airplane manufacturers and related industries use a virtual army of machine shops, tool and die shops, and the like to provide small parts. Large companies like Boeing will demand at least 30 if not 60 day or more terms from such "little guys" for the privilege of gaining their business. Factoring can be nearly required for many such shops to simply survive.

If you can learn from which vendors these large customers or government agencies purchase their products and services, you'll have a great list – and usually an enormous one at that – from which to prospect.

Referral Sources

Referrals can come from clients, acquaintances, neighbors, family members, and professionals who know of small companies in need of improved cash flow. On the list above we see "Accountants" and "Accounting and Bookkeeping Forms." Accountants and bookkeepers certainly know which of their clients have cash flow needs. So do bankers, financial planners, attorneys, insurance agents, and the like. When these people truly understand and appreciate how factoring can help (unfortunately many don't), and that you provide factoring services for very small businesses, they may be a source of referrals.

Your Established Network of Contacts

Now that you have an idea of how to "read" prospect lists and have begun to see the staggering potential number of clients out there, where do you begin? A good rule of thumb is to start with industries or companies in which you have some knowledge and/or contacts. If you've worked in high tech, for example, you may know component manufacturers, independent programmers, or web site developers who could be factoring prospects or at least sources of referrals.

What is your background? What do you know, what are your skills, and what do you enjoy? What types of businesses do you already know who need to improve their cash flow, and who invoice business or government customers? Who do you know that can point you toward potential clients? Begin here, and if you have enough contacts, this could be all the marketing you ever need to do, particularly if you're factoring part-time.

Those who work as factoring broker consultants often use a variety of marketing methods to find new clients: cold calling, bank referrals, internet marketing, direct mail, networking, and so on. However, the chances of your having a personal acquaintance, friend, neighbor, or family member who can benefit from small receivables factoring is high. Because so many people have started or are starting their own businesses, often from home and on a part-time basis, you very likely know at least one person – perhaps more – with his or her own small business. If they are selling to creditworthy business or government customers and are waiting roughly two weeks to two months to receive payment, they very likely are factorable.

We all know that word of mouth is the best (and least expensive) marketing. Such referrals are precisely what work best and lead most easily to very small prospects. People you know, who know you, tell people *they* know about your service.

Most people have a circle of acquaintances of approximately 200 people. Think of all the people you know, speak to, and with whom you are in some type of communication. Take a few minutes to review who is in your home and office address books, holiday card file, place of worship directory, Little League roster, and so on. When you add up all these people you know and who know you, you'll probably find a circle of around 200 people with whom you are on a friendly basis. How many of them have started a small business? Even more to the point, how many of them *know* someone in *their* circle of 200 who has started a small business?

Here the number of prospects for small factors grows quickly. When your 200 people know and understand what you do and the beneficial service you offer small business owners, you are very likely to find potential clients. Making sure people clearly understand what you do – and that you'll give them a finder's fee for leads that eventually fund – is the secret to gaining good referrals as a small factor. Social networking sites like Facebook, Google+, LinkedIn, and many others have expanded this type of networking exponentially.

To illustrate, I have a friend who read some of my material on factoring and came to understand what factoring does, how it works, and the types of companies it can benefit. He made a point of telling me, "I know a couple people who could really benefit from factoring." They were shirt-tail relatives and sure enough, owned small businesses with government customers and were in need of improved cash flow. Their businesses were relatively new, not bankable, and fit my parameters nicely. They would be desirable clients for nearly any small factor.

His relatives trust his recommendation to me as a factor because they know and trust him. He is comfortable referring my company because we have been friends for some time and he knows the level of service and value I provide. He'll make a nice commission for introducing us. But until he really understood factoring, he never would have put us together. He needed to learn, and if I hadn't provided him a rudimentary education in factoring, nothing would have happened.

Did I have to market to get these referrals? No. However, I did need to educate my friend, and he needed to grasp how factoring could help the people in his circle of acquaintances. Once that was accomplished, the referrals came with virtually no effort on my part at all. What's more, his time involved recommending my company to his relatives wasn't more than five minutes, if that.

I call this "acquaintance marketing," but it's really more educating than marketing. It costs very little or nothing, is done mostly by other people on your behalf, and brings you leads which are usually warm if not hot. You do need to screen these referrals quickly; often leads will be for unfactorable prospects because they sell to consumers, or some other reason. But compared to clients garnered by costly marketing campaigns, these leads are quite inexpensive if not free, take little time to qualify, and are exceptionally well-suited to factors of small receivables.

+ + +

The purpose of this chapter has not been to tell you which specific industries you should target for new business. The purpose has been to help you discern industries and companies that will need and welcome your service. This discernment comes from knowing the right questions to ask, the right people to use for referrals, and how to tap the unique resources, experiences, and contacts you already have. Especially if you start factoring part-time, these can garner your first clients and launch your factoring operation.

Part 3

Risk and Its Management

"There are inherent risks that you must understand, appreciate, and know how to minimize."

"Factoring risks can be managed with the proper tools."

7
Factoring Risks

If you are a highly risk-averse person – if you cannot bear the idea of ever losing any money at all – then most high yield investments including the stock market and factoring are not for you.

There are many people like this and they invest only in extremely safe instruments that yield very low returns, such as certificates of deposit, money market and savings accounts, and treasury bills. While their investments earn very little, they don't lose anything and that's how they prefer to live. No risk, no loss.

However, if you've read this far, my guess is you're not too likely to be one of these people. If your spouse or significant partner in life is such a person, however, that's another matter we'll address in the chapter, "Measuring Success and Determining What It Takes."

People who invest in the stock market understand its very nature is to have ups and downs over any period of time. Money may be made or lost any given year, quarter, month, week, day, even minute. While you want to increase the value of your stock portfolio, you realize that you will lose at least a little from some stocks at any time. The goal is to keep your overall position ahead: to make more than you lose. If you do, you are successful and your wealth grows.

While factoring is not subject to the daily dips and peaks that stocks are, like stocks there are inherent risks involved that you must understand, appreciate, and know how to minimize before you begin investing in invoices. Warren Buffett, one of America's best known investors, says, "Risk comes from not knowing what you are doing." This is especially true with factoring.

Factoring risks can be managed with the proper tools. Handled correctly, the high investment returns we saw earlier will remain right where you want them: in your bank account. If the risks are ignored or you believe you are somehow immune to them, you are likely in for a very rude awakening. As mentioned earlier, all factors experience financial losses. Therefore you must structure your operation so that a catastrophic loss can't happen, and any losses you do experience are small enough to absorb.

Two Risks You May Not Expect

Because of the nature of factoring small business receivables, I've observed two types of people are often attracted to it. There are unique risks each type faces, and everyone who acts as a factor shares certain common risks.

On one hand, the high returns from factoring attract people who are strongly motivated by high financial gain. These people like making money. They are often very successful in other investment or business ventures, know which strings to pull to ensure their funds will continue to grow, and are sometimes seen by others as having the Midas Touch. Often these people see factoring's unbelievable returns and want "their share" of that juicy pie.

The risk such people face is that of simple greed. There is a danger when greed – wanting nothing more than just making more and more money – is the primary focus. Not concerned with the good of the people their factoring service is established to assist, such people can easily lose the loyalty of their clients (if they ever had it in the first place).

What's more, when greed takes over their factoring practices can become cold and calculating. Quality of service, not to mention the quality of life and inner spirit, are compromised. Factoring simply becomes a means to a selfish end: making a lot of money. Those with a balanced perspective realize there is a lot more to life than just getting as rich as possible.

Greed is also a fast track to making bad factoring decisions. When a prospective client comes along that will provide exceptionally good returns but due diligence turns up some yellow or red flags, a factor's greed can lead him to accepting the client anyway. Unpleasant results too often follow.

In short, don't sell your soul, compromise a healthy perspective on life, or set aside good business judgment just to make big bucks. This risk is not apparent to most people early on.

On the other hand, the other unexpected risk lies at the opposite end of the spectrum. There are people who get into factoring because they sincerely want to help others, and the returns (while nice) are incidental. This is quite commendable but such a perspective has its own dangers.

These folks are great people yet are what cynics might view as saps: naïve, easily taken advantage of, an easy mark. Unfortunately certain people – too often dishonest clients with no integrity or scruples – can spot such people a mile away.

I have seen some very well-meaning people enter factoring and go overboard trying to help their clients. They give loans in addition to invoice advances, provide uncompensated extra service, give back rebates sooner than is wise, and generally knock themselves out for these clients. They not only go the extra mile – they go the third, fourth, and fifth miles.

These people run the high risk of being taken advantage of by clients and all too often end up losing a tidy sum when the client finally shows his or her true colors. And what hurts these kindly souls most is not just the money they lose: it is the loss of their innocence and trust in people. They're humiliated to have appeared so foolish, when in fact they did nothing morally wrong.

I have seen both of these scenarios – people in it only for the money who begin to rot inside, and genuinely nice people who get burned and lose their sweet outlook on humanity. For those who wish to factor successfully, they must find a middle ground where sound business practices, prudence and common sense overcome greed or excessive generosity.

When that middle ground is found you can successfully invest in receivables and not only make very good money, but truly help a number of people...and the world becomes a little better place.

That's what this book and others in *The Small Factor Series* are all about.

Four Common Risks You Face

Once you get beyond these personality-based risks there are other concerns that go with the territory. "What can go wrong when you buy receivables?" is a common question. Factors sooner or later can lose money from some (and if you do it long enough, all) of the following risks:

1. Nonpayment from customers.
2. Poor management of client businesses.
3. Personal events, usually in the lives of clients, that adversely affect their operation.
4. Fraud.

Let's look at each one.

1. Nonpayment

A customer doesn't pay one or more invoices you've purchased due to:

- A dispute with your client over product or services rendered.
- Inability to pay (inadequate cash on hand).
- Business closure.
- Bankruptcy.

Any of these can result in your not receiving payment for invoices you've bought. If you utilize proper due diligence described later in this book and in book 2 of this series and establish proper procedures, the chances of this occurring are lessened substantially. However, nonpayment does occur and factors deal with it on a fairly routine basis.

2. Poor Management

A client with poor management skills does not run his or her business wisely or efficiently. This can result in:

- Poor service or faulty products, and therefore dissatisfied customers who may be unwilling to pay.
- Debts resulting from a client's falling into arrears with financial obligations.
  - This can result in delinquent tax payments and overdue payables, which can impact factored receivables or other assets vital to the business if tax authorities or vendors lien or garnish these assets.
- Poor record keeping which can make their entire operation grossly inefficient and difficult for you to deal with.
- A client's business closes while factored invoices remain unpaid. Collecting these receivables can become difficult if the customer has little integrity as to its obligations.

Determining the management skills of your clients may forewarn you if this could be a problem.

3. Personal Events

Personal events in the life of a client or his/her close family members can impact the business, such as:

- Serious illness or injury.
- Divorce.
- Death of a family member or a person who is crucial to the business.

These are usually unforeseen occurrences and can happen to anybody. Proper procedures and risk management tools discussed later will go a long way toward protecting your investment.

4. Fraud

Fraud on the part of your client is an unhappy but real possibility you must acknowledge and guard against. Examples include:

A. The client receives payments for factored invoices and does not forward these payments to you. This is called "conversion" and is the most common fraud risk you'll face.

- Usually this occurs unintentionally by a client or a client's employee who doesn't realize a check they receive pays a factored invoice. When not caught quickly, however, such funds can be difficult to recover if a client's cash flow is very tight.
- When clients are extremely cash strapped they may deposit such checks knowing full well they were factored. This constitutes criminal fraud and you should let all new clients know from the start you and your attorney take such illegal acts very seriously.

B. The client factors invoices for which work has not been completed or product has not been delivered.

C. The invoice a client sends a customer has the client's address for remittance, but the invoice he provides the factor has the factor's address for remittance. This can occur if the factor funds invoices a client faxes the factor, rather than funding the original invoices the factor faxes or mails the customers.

D. The client instructs a customer that he is no longer factoring, and/or instructs a customer that payments for factored invoices should be re-routed to him. C and D can happen when:

- the client views his circumstances as dire and he justifies this action by reasoning he needs the money more than the factor (despite knowing that this is plainly fraud), and/or
- the client has become angered by something the factor has done and/or wants to terminate the relationship. Such terminations can only be done after the amount due the factor is paid.

E. Collusion on the part of the client and customer. Here the customer verifies that an invoice is approved for payment when in fact it has not been approved, and/or the individual providing verification does not have authority within the company to do so.

F. Collusion on the part of the client who creates and factors outright phony invoices with a bogus customer. Here the "customer" has no business or business relationship with the client at all and simply lies about the whole

transaction, usually because the client has provided incentive for doing so.
G. The client claims to own a company, but in fact there is no company and no customer. Phantom invoices – from a company that doesn't exist for a product or service never provided to a nonexistent customer – are created for you to buy.

Because purchasing invoices and receiving payments involve an ongoing relationship of trust and cooperation between factor, client, and customer, factors are vulnerable to a variety of types of fraud, as you can see. Again, taking proper precautions will prevent most of these from occurring. If fraud is attempted or occurs and you've implemented proper procedures, any loss you might experience can be kept to a minimum.

Is Factoring Worth the Risk?

With all these potential negatives, is factoring worth the risk? If you get burned by any of these experiences, especially for a large sum, you may understandably say it's not worth it. However if you take proper precautions, over the long haul the benefits certainly outweigh the risks or the people who make the high returns wouldn't stay in it!

Understand that while any of the above risks are real and can and do happen, when you run your factoring service properly the percentage of negative experiences are small compared to the positive ones. These dangers and pitfalls are described so you understand what is possible, and especially so you take steps to minimize the chances of them happening to you.

If something unfortunate does happen, the tools described in the next chapter will help you cope and keep your losses to a minimum. They will also help keep your perspective on business and life in general. Managed properly, the income you make from the vast majority of your factoring transactions will far and away overcome an occasional loss.

Let's look now at the many specific tools you can and should utilize to minimize your risk and keep your returns high. As you'll see, many of them involve simple common sense, cost little or nothing, and are easy to implement.

8
Risk Management Tools

The Gamble You Take

One might look upon investing in business receivables as a well calculated gamble, which managed properly, leans the odds of winning heavily in your favor.

Let's say you advance 80%, receive a 5% discount, and the average invoice you buy is $1,000. Each time you advance funds you are in essence "betting" $800 that the invoice will pay and when you are right, you "win" $50. If you are wrong, you lose $800 out of pocket plus the $50 discount you would have made.

Such "winnings" might not sound like much compared to the much larger "bets" you stand to lose. However, if you take all the precautions you should and perform the due diligence needed to minimize your risk, the chances of losing your advance actually become quite small. The $50 discounts you make on each advance quickly add up to far more than you would lose in a single "hit." Therefore when you stack your chances of winning in your favor this way, and limit your risk to fairly small amounts over a long period of time, the odds are very high that you'll come out ahead in the long run. Way ahead.

Bear in mind your chances of losing, especially losing large amounts, increase dramatically when:

a) you give advances for very big invoices, thereby putting a high amount of funds at risk per "hand," so to speak; and/or
b) you do not take due diligence precautions or use proper legal documents to protect your investment.

In other words, when you greedily or recklessly bet big money on a poor hand, you can't be surprised when you lose. In blackjack terms, don't split the two 5's you're holding. Or if you prefer poker, don't draw to an inside straight. People who know what they're doing just don't play that way.

Your Greatest Ally: Common Sense

Common sense doesn't cost a penny yet can save you thousands of dollars' worth of mistakes, time, and headaches. I never cease to be amazed at how little common sense some new factors use when they start.

As with any investment, it only makes sense to begin very slowly and gradually increase your exposure as you learn what you're doing. In other words, don't invest the bulk of your funds immediately or do so in only one or two invoices. Spoon feed yourself as you learn, slowly increasing the size of the bites as you take in the business and digest it. This is the best way to limit your risk at the very beginning.

Let's use two examples. Suppose a small factor named Steve has $50,000 in factoring funds and in a relatively short time he has two clients. One factors about $6,000 per month, the other around $4,000, leaving Steve a cushion for their growth and unexpected cash needs, and enough to fund new clients as they come along. His rates are steadily earning at least $500 per month for his investment from this single client.

Now the $4,000 client routinely factors around 20 invoices each month that average $200 in size. One month she takes on a new customer but this customer immediately closes his doors right after the client performs the service and invoices him. In short, this invoice goes bad and the customer never pays.

Steve's chances are high that he will recoup this loss from other invoices this client has. If Steve's on a recourse basis, his client is obligated to make up this loss with a fresh invoice or deducting what he's owed from reserves, rebates or future advances.

Even if Steve can't recoup this particular bad debt, a $200 loss is easily overcome by the $500 he is making monthly in discounts – not to mention the reserves he's steadily been putting aside from each discount earned. While this loss lowers his APR, it will have little if any impact on his factoring business. Steve recovers from this small loss without missing a beat.

On the other hand, another small factor named Nick also has $50,000 to invest, but he ignores the most basic risk management tool. He has just started out and booked his first client who wants to factor a $50,000 invoice. Against all common sense Nick invests all his funds in the only invoice of his single client's first customer.

The worst case scenario happens: the customer never pays and the client can't make up the money Nick's owed. He loses his $50,000 and has no more money to invest. Nick turns away from factoring with his head down, shoulders sagging, tail between his legs, and mutters that factoring is far too risky to be of any good to anybody. "Why did I ever do this in the first place, anyway?" he wonders.

Believe it or not Nick's scenario plays out all too often. People are seduced by the high yields (which are attainable when managed properly), and dollar signs spin in their eyeballs. The element of greed has taken its toll, overpowering the wisdom of common sense and simple prudence.

Over-concentration – the mistake Nick made of having too much of his money in one client, customer, and/or invoice – is far and away the biggest reason factors lose money and even go out of business, regardless of their size. I have seen small factors lose a few to several thousand dollars, and larger factors lose literally millions of dollars, from accounts in which they were over-concentrated. In the great majority of cases when factors close their doors or merge with another factor, the primary cause can be traced to losses where the factors were over-concentrated.

When you act wisely and develop – **and follow** – sound investment safeguards, you cannot have a catastrophic loss as Nick did. It's only when you don't develop, maintain, and follow these safeguards that your factoring investment comes into serious jeopardy.

What You Can Do

A large number of risk management tools are available which you can and must use. As with other investments, these tools do not guarantee you will never lose a dime, but they will highly reduce the likelihood of a loss, especially a serious loss. Used properly these tools will make the occurrence of a catastrophe virtually impossible. Ignored, you are courting disaster.

Remember that sooner or later all factors experience losses in the course of their operation. When they have not employed proper safeguards even one loss can knock them out of business, or simply incline them to get out of factoring. The trick is to keep negative experiences to a bare minimum. If you do, the income factoring makes will far exceed any losses.

The safeguards you can put in place fall into four[1] general categories:

1. Set financial limits.
2. Determine industries you will and will not factor.
3. Perform adequate due diligence.
4. Establish and build up reserves.

Let's look at each of these in more detail.

---

[1] A fifth safeguard is available to larger factors, but not small factors: credit insurance. There are insurance companies who insure against nonpayment of factored receivables. However, the volume required to obtain this insurance is usually well beyond the range of small factors. Those who plan to purchase large volumes of receivables should look into this, however.

1. Set Financial Limits

The financial limits you can and should set depend on the amount of funds you have and your tolerance for risk. These limits prevent you from becoming over-concentrated as discussed above. They should include the following:

- A specific maximum monthly volume amount you will fund for new clients.
- A specific maximum total volume amount you will fund for any client (his credit limit).
- The maximum increment by which you will increase a client's credit limit.
- The volume limit at which you will no longer factor clients, but broker them to larger factors or participate with another factor.
- The maximum volume amount you will fund for any customer. Bear in mind two or more clients might invoice the same customer.
- The maximum size invoice you will purchase.
- The maximum percentage of your capital you will invest in any one client, customer, or invoice.

One of the simplest means of avoiding a catastrophic loss is to limit your exposure to clients, customers, and invoices. These limits cap the size of any possible potential loss. Thus if the worst happens with a client's entire account and you've stayed within your guidelines, this will not mean the end of your operation. However being over-concentrated in any client, customer, or invoice can have very damaging effects as we saw in Nick's experience.

What's more, setting and staying within strict limits – especially with very low client volumes – has another benefit you might not realize. Avoiding larger invoice and client volume decreases your exposure to sophisticated criminals who are drawn to large amounts of money like bugs to a spotlight. While smaller volume is still vulnerable to crooked people trying to take you for a ride, the schemes tend to be less sophisticated.

However, you must always be diligent in your operations, regardless of its size. If you ever get an uneasy feeling about someone, follow your instincts and avoid them like the plague. "Just say no" can be very good advice in the factoring industry. Unfortunately, con men and women can be extremely skilled in gaining your trust and keeping it long enough to sting you. Vigilance must be part of your best defense.

2. Determine Receivables You Will and Will Not Factor

There are plenty of factor-friendly industries with ample prospective clients out there in need of your service. There's really no reason to risk your capital or waste your time on the marginal ones. Certain industries are more prone to factoring problems and unless you have personal experience or expertise in them, you are better off steering clear of them. They are discussed in the chapter, "Receivables to Avoid." Identifying desirable clients and customers, as well as referral sources, are discussed in the chapter, "Identifying and Locating Prospective Clients."

3. Perform Adequate Due Diligence

There are four general steps of due diligence. They include:

A. Determining if a client is one you wish to factor.
B. Determining if a customer is one you wish to factor.
C. Determining if a new invoice is one you wish to factor.
D. Taking action to secure payment on all invoices, especially overdue ones.

A. Client Due Diligence

Because you'll be purchasing the invoices of a client, what do you want to know about him or her? First and foremost clients need to be honest people with integrity. If you get the sense they might do something shady with any business transactions, chances are high you will be one of their first targets.

Unfortunately determining someone's honesty is pretty subjective and people often take time to show their true colors. However a quick search in public records, which are easily obtained online, will give evidence of judgments against them or a criminal record. These are not free and you'll need to determine how much you want to spend.

A knowledge of lien filings is also valuable. What is a lien? A lien (pronounced "lean") is a public record in which a person, business, or government who is owed money states publicly they are "first in line" in case the debtor defaults. Say a bank provides a $10,000 loan to a customer. The bank will file a lien called a UCC1 (which stands for Uniform Commercial Code) with the debtor's Secretary of State, claiming first rights to the assets of this customer.

If the customer defaults and declares bankruptcy, the bank will be in "first position" to collect its $10,000 from a judgment or bankruptcy settlement. Anyone who's filed a UCC1 chronologically after the bank is in "second position" and will get nothing from a settlement until the bank, in first position, receives all of its $10,000. If the debtor's assets equal only $9,000, the bank receives all of it and the second position holder gets zero.

Therefore, you want to know if a prospective client has any liens against him. If so, you need to make sure these liens are still valid. That is, if the lien holder is a bank, is the loan for which the lien was placed still owed or has it been paid in full? If it has been paid, the bank should release the lien and you'll be in first position once you file your UCC1. If another factor has a lien in place, the client is no longer factoring with them, and the client does not owe the factor anything, this lien should also be released. Filing and releasing a lien is just a matter of filling out a form (UCC1 for filing and UCC3 for releasing) and submitting it to the Secretary of State's office. In most states this can be done easily from the Secretary of State's web site.

If you find an existing and valid lien is already in place, you probably won't accept this client unless the lien holder will subordinate their lien to yours. But until they are paid in full, there is usually little incentive for lien holders to release their lien. Therefore your hope is to find no UCC1's in place with a prospective client.

Next it's important to make sure there are no tax issues or delinquencies. While you can be of great help getting such problems taken care of, you want to know about them before you have money invested in the receivables, not after.

UCC's, tax liens, and judgments are all public records and can be found from a variety of sources. These include courthouse records, credit reports, and private companies who research these records for a fee. UCC searches can be done from the web sites of many Secretaries of State as well.

What else do you want to know about a business in whose receivables you may be investing? It's helpful to know how long they've been in business and what experience the owner has in the industry. The more experience the owner has, chances are the more adept she'll be at her overall operation and the fewer potential problems there will be.

Also, why does the prospect want to factor in the first place? Good reasons to factor include meeting payroll, catching up or keeping up with taxes, expansion through new equipment, more staff, providing net 30 terms, obtaining discounts for cash, and keeping inventory levels up. These reasons usually indicate she is talking to you for the right reasons. If a prospect wants to factor poor paying customers who are nothing more than bad debts, she doesn't understand what factoring can really do, and is better off contacting a collection agency. Factors want to buy good receivables, not bad debt.

B. Customer Due Diligence

What do you want to know about new customers? Because they are the ones paying the invoices you're buying, you want to be sure they can and will pay. The best way to do this is to obtain a credit report on them from any of several credit reporting agencies. Dun & Bradstreet is among the best known, and there are numerous others whose costs are lower.

Most credit reports provide some kind of credit rating (usually a letter grade or numeric score) as well as public records information. These public records will show UCCs, judgments, and bankruptcies. If a customer has numerous judgments against him, this is an indication that others have had problems in the past serious enough to take to court. *Factoring Small Receivables,* book 2 in *The Small Factor Series,* has a complete chapter entitled "Credit Reports" which details the variety of information provided by various credit reporting sources and their costs.

You can also learn about customer payment patterns from your client's or other vendors' payment history. This payment history can be obtained from an aging report which bookkeepers or business owners using ordinary accounting software can produce. Programs such as QuickBooks provide these reports easily, and an aging report can often tell you very quickly whether or not you want to purchase invoices to specific customers.

C. New Invoice Due Diligence

Once you have accepted a client and at least the initial customer/s, you will receive invoices to be factored. What do you want to know about the invoices? Common sense – not rocket science – suggests you want to make sure:

- The service or product billed on the invoice has been provided and the customer is satisfied with its quality.
- The amount being charged is correct.
- The customer intends to pay.
- The payment will come from the customer directly to you, not to the client.

You also want to know the terms of the invoice: net 15, 30 45 etc., and whether the customer ordinarily pays within terms. It's a good idea, at least with new clients, to have the original invoice sent to you rather than directly to the customer. That way you can make sure your address is on the invoice so payment comes to you, and the invoice the customer receives is the one you sent.

Verifying the invoice – the first two points above – can be done with a phone call to the client, a letter signed by the customer, or by a signature on whatever document all parties agree will accomplish your purpose. These can be delivery receipts, work orders, bills of lading, time cards for temp agencies, the invoice itself, etc. The key ideas here are verification and accountability.

If you don't verify every invoice, which is common when you buy many invoices that are only a few hundred dollars in size, it is wise to do a spot check on the larger ones. That is, a few weeks after an invoice is sent, make a "courtesy call" on the customer to make sure the invoice was received, the customer has the correct remittance address (yours), and that payment is properly scheduled. Building rapport with customers this way can go a long way to getting paid when and for the amount you should.

D. Overdue Invoice Due Diligence

The last form of due diligence is to keep an eye on invoices that have not yet been paid and have slipped into the "late" category. When this happens what are you going to do? This is an important question you must discuss with your client because if this is not handled professionally your client's business can suffer and you may find getting your money back rather difficult.

Once you learn a customer's payment habits you will be able to discern which overdue payments need attention. A chapter in *Factoring Small Receivables* called "Preventive Maintenance" provides direction and procedures to follow in this matter.

4. Establish and Build Up Reserves

There are two types of reserve accounts that will provide further means of minimizing the consequences of a loss. The first is one you can start from day one, and its funds come from the discounts you earn.

Each time an invoice is paid, set aside a percentage of that income into a Bad Debt Reserve account. You may want to start it higher at first, perhaps ten or even twenty percent of each discount. Put these dollars into a savings or other interest bearing account that is separate from your regular operating account. As the account grows you might lower the amount taken from each discount earned to five or ten percent, or even less over time. The point is, consistently add to it so it will always be there to ease the sting if you ever experience a loss.

Never tap into this reserve for paying regular bills or giving advances. This is strictly a "rainy day" fund and is to be used to replenish capital only in the event of a loss. Having this money in reserve will add to your peace of mind and give you the satisfaction that you're running your factoring operation wisely.

The second type of reserve account to establish is an escrow reserve fund for each client you factor. Your factoring contract should make clear that you will do this, and you need to explain to prospective clients why and how this is done.

The reason is simple: if they ever have an invoice go bad you have an easy means of being repaid without negatively affecting their cash flow. Replacing a bad invoice with a new one might hurt their business, as can deducting amounts from advances or rebates. If money is set aside a little at a time, this will not cause them any hardship and becomes an insurance policy against bad debts from their customers.

How this can be done is also simple. Determine the amount of reserve you wish to establish, and keep a small portion of each advance until that reserve is reached. For example, say you want to have a reserve of 10% of a client's credit limit. If he has a credit limit of $10,000 that means his escrow reserve will build up to and remain $1,000.

To get there, withhold a specified amount, perhaps 5% of an invoice's face value, from each advance. For example, say you give an 80% advance. On a $1000 invoice, you will advance 75% or $750 and put 5% or $50 into the escrow reserve. Continue to set aside this 5% from each advance until the reserve has reached the $1,000 mark. Once it's there, you stop withholding the 5% and still have money to cover unpaid invoices. If the reserve needs to be used to cover an unpaid invoice, resume setting aside the escrow reserve deduction until it's reached again. When the client ceases factoring, give him whatever balance is in the escrow reserve account.

Having an escrow account has saved the hides of many of my factoring clients over the years; while few resist the idea, when its purpose and method are clearly explained many see the wisdom of doing this and are happy to have it. The escrow reserve account need not be a separate bank account, but simply a separate liability account in your bookkeeping software's chart of accounts.

+ + +

As you start your factoring investments or business I strongly urge you to make a list of the policies you will follow to minimize your risk. It will go a long way to help you determine if you will accept a new client, customer, or invoice. Private parties who may wish to invest in you will also gain confidence when you provide a printed policy. Creating and following sound procedures will help you run a tight ship and enable you to sleep very soundly at night.

The chapter "Preparations" contains a sample policy statement I have made for my factoring business. You need not follow this form or my specific policies since this is provided only as an example; however, it has worked well for me.

9

Receivables
to Avoid

The six industries or types of receivables wisely avoided by new small factors with no experience in them are:

1. Construction Receivables
2. Medical Receivables
3. Trucking Receivables
4. International Receivables
5. Consumer Receivables
6. Non-government Purchase Order Funding

Let's look at the reasons for steering clear of each of these.

Construction Receivables

This industry has many contractors, sub-contractors, and sub-sub-contractors who could benefit greatly from factoring. In fact prospective construction deals are among the easiest to find. The hard part is finding a factor who will fund them.

Most larger factors avoid construction and those who fund them usually have worked as contractors themselves, or have many years of experience financing them. If you can find a factor willing to fund construction receivables and you can broker such deals to them, you can do quite well. However, even those factors who fund construction do so with clearly defined restrictions and turn away a large number of presented deals.

The problems with construction deals are as follows:

- Most sub-contractors are not paid for their work until the contractor is paid by the bank, building owner, or whoever is funding the project. If there is a delay in payment at the higher level (which is actually very common), the sub – and the factor awaiting payment – can be hung out to dry for a very long time. This same problem can also occur with other industries when the client is doing subcontracted work, so always find out if invoices you buy are subject to the customer receiving payment first. Such invoices are good to factor.

- Many construction jobs involve progress billing, in which payments are made upon completion of specific steps of a job. Factoring a progress billing means the client seeks advances as the steps are completed, perhaps every two weeks or every month. When the job is completed payment may be withheld for a variety of reasons: wrong materials used, the work may not conform to code or specifications – you name it. The work must be corrected before funds are released, and correcting the problem usually means additional cost. However, payment will be only for the amount originally contracted. You have little control over this and as you can see, this is an extremely risky proposition for the factor.

- If another subcontractor on the same project has a dispute with the contractor, he can easily slap a mechanic's lien on the entire project until he is paid and satisfied. This can delay funding for everybody else and you have absolutely no control over it.

- Smaller construction companies are often financially precarious and their closure rate is high. If this is the customer paying your client's invoices, your risk is much higher than with more financially sound debtors.

- A common game in the construction industry is to simply not pay for work completed. The unscrupulous people who play this game simply refuse to pay for work performed, usually by a sub, and then just say "sue me." They're betting the sub is too small to take them to court, doesn't have the means to collect the legitimately owed payment, and some unsavory people in the construction industry simply run their businesses this way. It's a harsh world, so stay out of it.

As with nearly everything, one exception within the construction industry can be argued as reasonable to factor. Some small factors will accept a small unbonded[1] sub-contractor who does specific work for a large, established, and reputable general contractor. The sub might be a roofer, for example. When the contractor is financially sound, has been in business for some time with an honest reputation, and is not waiting to be paid before paying the sub, this type of customer can be a lower risk. Just be sure the contractor is not awaiting payment himself, has several properties or other assets to ensure his own financial stability, and has a good history of dependable payment cycles.

Third Party Medical Receivables

Third party medical receivables are another commonly avoided industry. Bear in mind that medical receivables which are paid by hospitals and credit worthy businesses (second party) are generally quite desirable and most factors welcome them. So what's the problem with other medical receivables?

Medical receivables which are submitted to third party payers (insurance companies, Medicare, Medicaid, and the like), as well as private payments made by patients or their families, are the ones to avoid. Insurance companies require that medical bills be properly "coded" before they are paid. That is, each medical procedure by each type of medical specialist has its own specific code.

Have you ever been to the doctor and signed a form which describes the treatment you received? If you look at it carefully, you'll see that all the procedures – physical exams, vaccinations, specific treatment for a particular injury or illness, and so on – have number codes next to them. The procedure or treatment the doctor performed for you is checked with the charges written next to it.

---

[1] If a subcontractor is bonded, the bonding company will be in first position ahead of any creditor in case a dispute or problem arises.

This bill is then submitted to the insurance company who checks to make sure the codes are correct. Those making these entries are trained to look for coding errors. If errors are found, payment is refused and the bill must be resubmitted correctly. If the codes are correct, the insurance company pays a specific amount for the procedure.

To make it interesting, the amount paid is usually not the full amount charged and depends on the policy's coverage with each particular insurance company. Many carriers pay different amounts for identical procedures and you have no way of knowing what those amounts are until you've dealt with a particular insurance company for a while.

Now if you were to factor such receivables, you need to know the correct code for each procedure, especially those that aren't pre-printed on the form, plus the percentage the particular insurance company being billed will pay for that procedure. When you consider that each medical specialty has its own codes, and each medical practice bills numerous insurance companies for multiple procedures, and that the entry clerks are looking for coding and other mistakes, you can see that you have opened a can of worms if you have no experience whatsoever in this field.

One more thing. Insurance companies require that medical bills be submitted electronically, which means you have to have very specific medical coding software that is often a separate business all by itself.

But it gets even worse, believe it or not. If a medical invoice received by the insurance company is found to be coded incorrectly, they not only don't pay it; they usually simply ignore it and don't tell anyone. The onus is on the medical billing company – in this case you – to track the payments and follow up on bills that are underpaid or not paid at all. In either case you rarely talk with the same insurance representative each time you call, and tracking such bills can become a nightmare without trained staff handling them.

Thus medical receivables quickly go far beyond the scope of small factor investors, and you're wise to simply broker medical receivables paid by third parties altogether. Larger factoring companies specialize in this niche and like construction, you can do quite nicely brokering such deals. But factor them yourself? No thanks.

Government medical payments like Medicare have similar problems and add the layer of government regulations to the mess. Further, I have seen Medicare payments cover an invoice, then be deducted from a later payment for a different invoice for reasons known only to the clerk who made the deduction. Does tracking such receivables sound like fun? Not to me.

Trucking Receivables

Trucking is an industry that a number of factors, both large and small, welcome. These people have usually been working with transportation receivables for some time and are familiar with the paperwork and finer points involved in this niche. It's not unusual for many of them to be former truckers themselves. And that's precisely why they're well suited for it: they know everything needed to make (or not make) money far better than those whose only experience with the trucking industry is seeing big semis on the highway.

These receivables are more complicated than others because they involve:

a) the trucking company who is paid to haul the load (and factors the invoice);

b) the business from which a load originates who wants the cargo moved;

c) often (but not always) a brokerage firm which puts the two together and establishes the price, receives payment from the customer after the load is delivered, and in turn pays the trucker;

d) a destination which may include a fourth company, or at least another individual who receives and signs for the load when it's delivered.

As you can probably infer from this number of parties involved, trucking receivables involve a lot of paperwork. Each party wants its own particular set of documents, all of which must be properly filled out and signed before each is satisfied. If any one document is missing or incomplete or improperly filled out, payment for the load can be held up for quite some time.

This can be very annoying to say the least, and make the delay in receiving payment a very long and tedious wait. When everything is filled out correctly and transactions run smoothly, payments are usually dependable. However, you must know what documents will be required by each party, what information each looks for on every document, and be able to catch errors before you advance funds. If you don't, you can wait a long time to get paid, or even be taken advantage of by less than honest individuals. When such people are on the road much of the time, they can be very hard to locate.

If the first two parties mentioned above are the only ones involved in a trucking client's receivables, trucking can be pretty straightforward and not that difficult. However, many trucking firms, even very small operations with only one or two rigs, often take jobs from brokers and the parties involved can easily be all four mentioned.

As you can imagine, people involved in trucking often live a somewhat rugged life. Regular travel, handling big rigs, and dealing with life on the road, drivers, and/or employees can make for some stressful moments for anyone associated with these receivables. If you don't have fairly thick skin and must learn as you go, this industry can lead to some less than gentle moments.

Further, transportation factoring is very competitive because the trucking industry is quite dependent on factoring. As a result, trucking factors usually give higher advances and earn lower discounts than those funding other industries.

In short, if you have no experience in transportation and want to turn your money quickly, consistently, and with lower risk, trucking is probably not the best industry for you.

As stated earlier, there are simply a lot of other good receivables out there needing your attention that are better suited to the portfolio of a rookie small factor. If you have years of experience with trucking, or at least can work closely with and learn from a factor who has such experience, you might do quite well factoring small trucking receivables. If not, I suggest you avoid the potential headaches and risk.

International Receivables

International receivables involve transactions between companies in two different countries. For an American factor, this can be an American client and foreign customer, a foreign client and an American customer, or a client and customer in two countries outside the U.S.

Numerous means of financing such receivables are available. Like trucking, very specific documents are required – each of which must be completed properly. When letters of credit (guarantees made by a financial institution) are used, which is quite common, a separate financial institution in each country is needed to enable shipment and reception of goods. These transactions are rather complex and can leave someone new to international factoring (or new to factoring in general) with his/her head spinning trying to understand everything involved. Rather than go into detail explaining the intricacies of international factoring, suffice to say...don't bother funding them.

Such receivables are quite a bit larger than small factors can manage with the funds they have available, and this point alone usually prevents them from entering as a funding source. Like brokering medical receivables, if you are properly positioned with an international factor and potential client companies involved in the import/export trade, you can make quite good commissions brokering such transactions. However, don't try to fund these unless you have extensive experience in the field and a very hefty bank balance. Again, there are much better places to invest your money.

Consumer Receivables

By definition factoring is the discounted purchase of business to **business** or business to **government** receivables. There are many consumer receivables out there but these are outside the arena of ordinary factoring transactions.

Consumer receivables include credit card payments which are essentially factored transactions at low rates and very high advances provided by the credit card companies. This is the vast majority of consumer factored transactions and credit card companies' rates and advances are too low for factors to compete with. Further, consumer payment defaults are generally higher than business payment defaults and collecting consumer defaults can be quite difficult. They're not something a small factor wants to pursue.

There are other types of consumer receivables such as contracts for home appliances. Here, a store selling a refrigerator, for example, provides financing. This may be done in cooperation with a finance company, or the store itself may finance the consumer. The common practice is to take a down payment and then receive monthly payments. Again, this is more in the bailiwick of consumer finance companies and department or appliance stores. These are not the kinds of receivables that provide the high return or low maintenance we small factors can easily find elsewhere.

Non-Government Purchase Orders

Non-government Purchase Order funding stretches across just about all industries and is the final area for small factors to avoid. Let's see how it works and why we don't want it.

When business customers place an order for a product or service, they often do so with a document called a Purchase Order. A P.O. is simply a piece of paper that says, in effect, "My company wants to buy X number of products or services from your company for X price."

The Purchase Order is given to the vendor who then fills the order. He will create the number of products or perform the service on the P.O., finish the job, whereupon the customer now owes the money. The vendor creates an invoice (usually with the P.O. number included) and sends the invoice to the customer for payment. This is a very common and standard way of doing business. Once the invoice is prepared, the need for the factor occurs assuming the vendor (client in this case) needs improved cash flow. But let's take just one small step back.

Suppose a fairly new bar stool manufacturing company receives a Purchase Order from a large furniture store chain, who likes their new line of bar stools. The furniture chain places a test order for 100 bar stools.

The manufacturer assembles the bar stools from wood and leather materials on hand, the stools are shipped to the furniture store chain, and the invoice is created and sent. Now the manufacturer waits 60 days for payment in accordance with the terms this customer required. Large national chains often require longer terms like this for the privilege of having their business.

The furniture company receives the bar stools, places them in stores, and finds they sell like hotcakes. They are so happy with them they decide to order 500 more and require the new order be delivered in three weeks. Meanwhile they still have four weeks in which to pay the first invoice.

However, because the manufacturer is relatively new in business, not only did the first order deplete all his wood and the leather materials needed to make the bar stools, he does not have the capital to purchase more raw materials for the large second order until the first invoice is paid. What can he do? He must either:

a) refuse the order (not a good idea),
b) factor the current invoice (what he should have done in the first place but didn't), or
c) find some means of funding the new purchase order.

As we'll soon see, factoring the current or other present invoices is the best choice, but too often the P.O is all the client thinks of because it is immediately at hand. Therefore, often close to a panic, the manufacturer looks frantically for someone who will fund the P.O. – and usually can't find any takers. We'll see why in a moment.

If he can find a P.O. funding company this is theoretically how the transaction takes place. The vendor (client) provides a copy of P.O. to the funding source, who determines the order is legitimate, the furniture store chain is a credit worthy customer, and the client will be able to fulfill the order with financial help.

The client then places an order for new raw materials needed to make the bar stools. The suppliers' bills for the raw materials are paid directly by the P.O. funding source (an advance is not given to the client to pay the suppliers). The raw materials are shipped to the client, who then makes the 500 new bar stools.

When the bar stools are completed and ready to ship, the funding source engages a factor who will purchase the new invoice created. Alternately, the P.O. funder may act as the factor itself. If another factor is involved, the factor pays the P.O. funding source what was advanced plus its discount, and that amount is considered part of the advance on the new invoice. This invoice is then treated as a regular factored transaction.

Now, this sounds quite smooth and when it works properly, it can be. However, do you see where problems can develop? There are many potential "flies in the ointment." The company placing the order may change its mind before the order is filled and:

a) want a different number of products than originally ordered,
b) want a different product or model,
c) want a different delivery date, or
d) may cancel the order all together.

If any of these things happen and you've advanced funds for raw materials that are no longer needed or now aren't the correct materials, what happens?

If the materials can be used for other orders, those invoices can be factored and you'll be okay. However if the materials you've paid for are not needed for other orders or were very specialized for this order, that inventory may not be useable. Thus no invoice will be generated to cover the materials you've paid for, and you've paid for useless product. In this scenario the client may have a very hard time paying you (he couldn't afford the supplies in the first place and now has no sale from which to pay you back) and there will be no invoice for another factor with which to buy out the funds you invested. Not good.

This is why most companies specializing in P.O. funding usually do not advance on P.O.'s for which the product must be assembled: the risk is too high. Rather, they advance on P.O.'s for which the client's supplier is drop-shipping a product already assembled – books or office products, for example – not materials for bar stools.

Now I must quickly point out that virtually all orders placed by governments entities (school districts, cities, counties, states, and federal agencies) are made with purchase orders. By law the government is required to pay when it issues a Purchase Order, and often this P.O. is the only verification you need or will get with government receivables. As long as the client hasn't created a phony government P.O. or converts a payment, these are usually very solid (though sometimes quite slow paying) transactions. Some factors even specialize in government receivables as their niche, while others reject them because they may take longer to pay (two to six months is quite possible) than the factor desires.

Unfortunately, businesses are not bound to honor purchase orders the way governments are, and as you can see, providing non-government P.O. funding can be quite risky.

The best thing to do when you are asked to fund a non-government Purchase Order is to find if there are other current invoices which can be factored. Often there are and advancing on these will provide the capital needed to purchase the raw materials for a new P.O. Once that order becomes an invoice, it can be factored to pay for future orders, and so on. The extra P.O. funding expense to the client and risk to the factor are avoided.

Regular invoice factoring is much safer for you and much less costly for the client than non-government Purchase Order funding. With non-government P.O. funding, the client receives no advance other than having the raw materials paid for, pays a charge for the P.O. funding, plus another discount (and might receive a very small remaining advance) when the invoice is factored.

If you can make clients aware that factoring is far better for everyone than P.O. funding, you can save them a lot of money and yourself a lot of grief.

Other Receivables to Avoid

Some Property Management Companies

Service companies such as janitors, lawn services, window washers, painters, handymen and the like are often excellent clients. Some provide services to apartment complexes whose bills are paid by property management companies. While some management companies pay their bills in a timely and professional manner and make fine customers, a good many others unfortunately can be a royal pain when it comes to getting paid.

The bad ones often ignore your notice of assignment and pay the client directly (despite your frequent attempts to correct this), regularly pay very slowly, and often short pay invoices or take deductions for undisclosed reasons. Moreover, reaching the right person to answer your follow up calls can be next to impossible; phone calls never being returned is quite common.

Dealing with on-site managers is often no better. I once had an apartment manager refuse to talk to me about a slow payment because I wasn't the one who did the work. Despite the fact that I made it clear I was directed by my client (who did the work) to make the call, in this person's mind he was fully justified in his reasoning because I was not the one who had personally provided the service. Talking to him was like talking to a wall, only a wall is smarter.

The many frustrations when dealing with apartment management companies and on-site managers put them on my list of receivables to avoid.

Most Insurance Companies

Receiving payment from many insurance companies closely parallels the experiences of dealing with unresponsive apartment management companies. Insurance companies are masters at not paying what their customers expect in claims, and what their vendors expect for services rendered.

Working through the phone maze to reach the correct person is practically impossible: After being directed to numerous extensions which in turn refer you to another extension, the final person you think may actually answer your inquiry all to often results in being told, "He's not here now," "She's on vacation," "He's gone this week," "She's in a meeting for the rest of the day," and/or "Call a different extension" ad nauseum. If you do actually talk to someone they will usually not give any commitment of when or how much an invoice is going to be paid. Further, if (not necessarily when) an insurance company finally does pay an invoice, the payment can be horribly slow to arrive.

Insurance companies which cover particular industries also have very specific practices that can make factoring quite difficult. For example, insurance payments for auto glass claims require that a phone call be made for every single invoice submitted. If a call is not made, the insurance company just doesn't pay it. These invoices are usually fairly small and getting paid for every single invoice is quite labor intensive. Such high maintenance receivables are not something you normally want to buy.

Before funding any invoices to an insurance company, be sure you completely understand the complete runaround....er, procedure...you can expect before getting paid. Once you do, you'll probably come to the conclusion that funding these receivables is not worth the trouble.

Sub Contractors' Invoices on a "Pay When Paid" Basis

As mentioned in the section on Construction, many subcontractors work for companies on a "pay when paid" basis. Arrangements like this in other industries are also not usually favorable for factoring because you're pretty far down the food chain and have little leverage for getting paid in a timely manner.

For example, say a small glass installation company does work for a large national glass company who has contracts with big customers such as Radio Shack. Radio Shack has a local store whose glass door is broken and needs to be replaced. They call the national glass company to repair it, who in turn subcontracts the job to the small local installer.

The installer does the work, submits his invoice to the large glass company, and the large company submits its invoice to Radio Shack. However, Radio Shack might be extremely slow to approve the paperwork and eventually takes 120 days to pay the contractor. If the subcontractor is on a "pay when paid" basis, he is going to likely wait an *additional* 30 to 60 days *after* Radio Shack pays the contractor, because the contractor requires these terms from his subcontractors. Thus the small glass installer could wait as much as 150 to 180 days to get paid after completing the job, and neither he nor his factor can do much of anything about it.

This is not an uncommon practice and you are wise to learn very early if prospective clients are on a pay when paid basis with customers they want to factor. You want to factor companies whose customers pay on a regular 15, 30, or 45 day basis *regardless* of when they get paid.

Governments in Trouble or with Payment Procedural Issues

Until the Great Recession, government receivables were generally safe and desirable investments for nearly all factors. If a client went to a factor saying he was paid by a government agency, approving these receivables was and still often is a very routine matter.

However, in recent years many government bodies have fallen on difficult times. California is well known for being tens of billions of dollars in the red and has occasionally resorted to paying its bills with IOUs because it did not have funds in the bank to meet its obligations. Other states are running deficit budgets, slashing programs, heatedly debating raising taxes, and desperately trying to balance their budgets, upsetting just about everyone in the process. Those facing serious budget deficits often pay their bills much more slowly than they used to, to the point where taking many months to pay with no definite payment date in sight is putting some of their smaller vendors out of business.

Additionally, we hear about counties and cities declaring bankruptcy, often when expensive spending projects preceded a serious drop in revenues. As a result, factors need to do much more research about the stability and economic health of government bodies before assuming that buying receivables to them is a good idea. Unfortunately, credit reporting agencies do not have data on government agencies like they do on businesses, so learning about a government's financial health and timeliness of payments can be rather difficult.

On another level, while some government agencies are excellent payers and have impressive bill paying systems and web sites where vendors can see clearly when they will be paid, others are remarkably inefficient. For many vendors, knowing when and how much they will be paid is nothing less than a crapshoot. Poor computer payables software, cumbersome and inefficient invoice approval processes, and cuts to programs and departments make getting paid a real challenge for these vendors. Do your homework regarding a government's financial health, and look for historical payment trends for at least the last few years from prospective clients' government customers, before you agree to factor those invoices.

Fundamentals for Factors

Part 4

Moving Forward

"What are you looking for in an investment or business? Will factoring provide this for you?"

"How do you measure success?"

10

Is Factoring Right for You?

Thus far we have considered the basics of factoring transactions, the returns that are possible, the risks involved, how to manage or avoid the risks, and receivables to leave alone. Now it's time to determine if factoring as an investment or a business is the right move for you personally. We'll consider two important issues:

1. What are you looking for in an investment or business?
2. Will factoring provide this for you?

What Are You Looking for?

The first and most obvious question is this: what are you looking for? That is, can you identify three or four specific characteristics of an investment or business that are absolute requirements for you?

For example, a man named Gene has worked in the corporate world for the last few years and has come to realize that's not the career path he wants. He has spent quite some time searching for a venture that will fulfill very specific needs he has identified as most important in his life. He has narrowed these needs down to three specific requirements. His new venture must:

1. Have low initial capital expense.
2. Allow him to be home-based.
3. Allow him to start part-time.

If various business models don't meet all three requirements, Gene discards them and keeps looking. Let's see how factoring measures up to his needs.

1. Low initial capital expense means Gene doesn't want to have a large outlay of funds at launch to get his business up and running.

   For example, purchasing a franchise or pre-existing business will require some significant upfront money. An initial franchise fee (tens of thousands of dollars or more), or a large down payment to purchase an existing business will be required before he can even open his doors. These will quickly be followed with monthly royalty discounts to the franchisor, or monthly payments for the remainder of the business note debt. Therefore Gene has concluded a franchise or pre-existing business will not meet his first requirement.

   By the way, factoring franchises do exist and we suggest you carefully research them before "signing on the dotted line." Perform each of the following steps if you are considering a factoring franchise:

   A. Determine the true value of the "name" you're buying. Have you ever heard of it before? If not there's probably little value in the name to potential clients, referral sources, or you.

   B. Find out if protected territories are provided.

   C. Call several franchisees (and not just the ones whose phone numbers the franchisor provides) to discover the percentage who are truly enthusiastic about their affiliation with the franchise.

   D. Consider whether you'll need the franchisor's continued support over time. You will continue to pay royalties for this support forever. Will you still need it in a year?

   E. Ask how much freedom you will have in determining your rates and advances. If you have little or no discretion, how will you fare next to an independent competitor who can set any advance or discount he chooses?

F.   Finally, determine the franchise fee and monthly royalty amounts, and calculate if you would significantly improve your return and profitability by being an independent small factor. That is, would investing this money in clients' invoices, rather than spending them on these fees, improve your position? Franchise and royalty fees are expenses on your Income Statement; if you invest these funds in invoices, they are assets on your Balance Sheet. Would you rather have performing assets that grow or nonperforming expenses that continue forever?

Becoming a small independent factor meets Gene's first need of low initial capital expense. By starting very slowly and with no franchise fees to pay, Gene has no capital expenses whatsoever. His startup expenses will be very small and his working capital can immediately be used for early marketing efforts and purchasing his first client's invoices. This will provide relatively quick income without having to wait many months or even years to see a return on investment, as is true with most traditional businesses.

So being a small independent factor meets Gene's first requirement quite nicely.

2.   Gene wants to work out of his home to a) be more available for his family, b) save the expense, time and headache of a commute, and c) have a more flexible schedule.

I recommend most people start as a small factor from home. Preferably you will have a spare bedroom or separate office space, but you can start with just a desk in your "work corner" if necessary. By starting from home you avoid the expense of monthly rent, the long-term obligation of a lease, and with proper direction from a professional accountant, you may be able to deduct your home office space from your taxes.

So Gene's requirement #2 goes hand-in-hand with being a small factor.

3. Gene presently has a full-time job and must start factoring part-time.

    No problem. Factoring is flexible enough that you can begin part-time if you prefer or must, or full-time if you have adequate funds.

    Starting part-time will give you the time and psychological space to get your office set up and procedures in place. You'll be able to do some low-key marketing; just telling your friends what you're doing may bring in that first client. And you won't feel the pressure to start making full-time income which can very likely prevent you from making an expensive rookie mistake. As stated earlier, start with very small clients, learn what you're doing with them, and increase gradually.

    So does factoring small receivables meet requirement #3 for Gene? Absolutely.

25 Possible Requirements

What are some other possible prerequisites people considering a new venture might have? Below are 25 requirements that a group of people might collectively put together, which as you can see include Gene's three needs. Most people have at least one or two on their list while others may have as many as a dozen. Circle the number next to any of the requirements you identify as your own. If yours are not included add them in the blank lines provided at the end.

My new venture must:

1. Have initial low capital expense.
2. Be home-based.
3. Allow me to be in charge of the decisions (be "captain of the ship").
4. Have flexible hours or hours that I choose.
5. Allow me to start part-time.
6. Allow me to start or become full-time.
7. Be possible to perform with the presence of a disability I have.
8. Not interfere with family or other responsibilities.

9. Allow for the presence and interruptions of children.
10. Allow me to run the business with a spouse or family member.
11. Allow me to run the business alone.
12. Allow me to hire staff as needed or desired.
13. Be suitable as an add-on to an existing business I already have.
14. Allow me to start with $_____ in capital.
15. Be able to create a dependable income of $_____.
16. Provide a needed service that is beneficial to others.
17. Utilize my background, skills, and experiences.
18. Provide ongoing challenges and not become another "boring job."
19. Have training and/or support available.
20. Have minimal or no training costs.
21. Have minimal or no ongoing support costs.
22. Require no special equipment, tools or machinery.
23. Require no inventory.
24. Require no particular clothing style (dress code, uniforms, etc.).
25. Allow the presence of my pet/s.
26. _____
27. _____
28. _____
29. _____
30. _____

Will Factoring Provide What You Need?

Let's briefly review each item in the above list. If you've identified others and written them in the blank lines, determine if being a small factor will meet them as well.

1. Have low initial capital expense.
As we saw with Gene, working as an independent small factor will cost virtually nothing to get started, other than the operating capital you need to buy invoices. Your available funds can be put to work immediately and will quickly generate income.

2. Be home-based.

Again, this is the recommended way to start. If you want an outside office that's certainly up to you but it will involve monthly expenses and probably a lease. If you outgrow your home office you can always move up, and by then you should be able to absorb the cost of rent.

3. Allow me to be in charge of the decisions (be "captain of the ship").

As the boss of your small factoring company or only decision maker for your receivables investment, you make virtually every decision that affects your capital and company. You will create discount and advance rates that are competitive and provide good and valuable service, and you will decide what these are. If you want to make decisions, rest assured: you definitely will.

4. Have flexible hours or hours that I choose.

The hours of factoring are quite flexible. You do need to be available during normal business hours if you're doing face-to-face or telephone marketing; however if you choose other means of finding clients, that's not necessarily required. You'll also need to speak with your clients from time to time, as well as their customers for some invoice verifications – and this may need to be done at specified hours. Once an account is set up, however, a great deal of the servicing can usually be done at your convenience.

5. Allow me to start part-time.

Again as we saw with Gene, this is the recommended plan.

6. Allow me to start or become full-time.

Starting full-time can be done as long as you don't invest a large amount of funds too quickly, before you learn what you're doing. The two main requirements for going full-time are having enough time and adequate capital. Using the charts we saw in the chapter "Return on Your Investments," you can quickly see how much capital you'll need to make the full-time income you require.

7. Be possible to perform with the presence of a disability I have.

Factoring is primarily a people and relationships business, with some office procedures and tasks thrown in. If you are good with people, fair minded, determined to do what is helpful for others **and** good for your business, and have good common sense as it applies to business and finances, you'll conquer the most important parts. Keeping track of your accounts and bookkeeping is the office part of it. Can you – or can someone on your behalf – use a computer? Use the phone? Prepare and transfer funds? Make bank deposits? Those need doing as well.

8. Not interfere with family or other responsibilities.

If you are working part-time, your factoring hours will be pretty flexible. You may need to allot at least some of your time for making invoice verifications and client contact during regular business hours. Other than that, when you work this business is up to you and can be worked around family or other responsibilities.

9. Allow for the presence and interruptions of children.

This is one of the most common reasons people want to work at home. The frequency and duration of kids' interruptions depend somewhat on their ages. Infants need tending when they need tending, and trying to close a new client with a wailing baby in the background can be a challenge. However, most people are pretty understanding about babies and having one can actually provide some "connections" with business contacts who are parents, grandparents, or who just love little ones.

You need to teach small children and older kids definite boundaries about your work time and space. Be consistent, do what you say you will do, and don't steal time you've promised them to use for work. Having kids around will require you to be self-disciplined and to budget your time. It can also be fun for you and provide a unique learning environment for your kids. Don't expect it to work perfectly all day every day; but handled properly, being around your family while you work can be a source of great satisfaction.

10. Allow me to run the business with a spouse or family member.

Small factoring operations are ideally suited to couples or families who work well together. If you are a good team and each person understands his or her role, as well as the others' roles, you can enjoy working this business for quite some time. There are many examples of couple-run or family-run factoring organizations. The only down side is carving time out for vacations. If there's no one left to tend to clients in your absence, getting away for more than a week or two can get complicated. While you can certainly take your laptop or other mobile device and work away from home, you're still working and may miss a sense of total rest and relaxation that being *completely* away affords.

11. Allow me to run the business alone.

If you prefer working alone or your spouse or family members have no interest in factoring, that's fine too. Again, taking time for vacation can prove to be one of the more tricky maneuvers for those who work solo.

12. Allow me to hire staff as needed or desired.

Realizing the need for help creeps up when you want to take a vacation as just mentioned, or when you begin to feel overwhelmed with the amount of business you have and the amount of time you have to do it. Having staff creates a whole new dimension to running a business and you need to consider this carefully before you take on help.

It's a good idea to think, when you are just starting, how large you really want to become. If you're happy with a cottage-industry type of business or only intend to factor as a part-time investor, determine how many clients you can manage with the time you will devote to factoring, and don't take on more than that. If you want to grow as much as possible, you will certainly need staff eventually.

13. Be suitable as an add-on to an existing business I already have.

Many successful business owners learn about factoring and add it to their existing enterprise. Some types of professions lend themselves quite well to this, such as bookkeepers, accountants, financial advisors, attorneys, and others who work with money.

Others in a variety of industries, particularly those which fit into niche factoring categories – consultants to nearly any industry, manufacturing, service businesses, and trucking, medical, or construction – all know the unique circumstances of their trades well enough to integrate a factoring arm into their operation.

14. Allow me to start with $_____ in capital.

As we saw in the chapter "Return on Your Investments," you need *some* money with which to purchase invoices, so a zero here probably won't work…unless you have at least one investor who believes in you. Many of today's most successful factors started with nothing but OPM (Other People's Money).

One consideration any time you use OPM: what happens if borrowed funds are lost to bad debt? To what terms of repayment or non-repayment will you both agree *before* the money is borrowed? Whatever your agreement, put it in writing and have both parties sign.

15. Be able to create a dependable income of $_____.

Again, refer to the chapter "Return on Your Investment" and its charts. How much you make in discounts depends on the amount of funds invested in receivables.

16. Provide a needed service that is beneficial to others.

The first chapter of this book provides an explanation of how this service is of value to and needed by a huge number of small businesses. You not only benefit the small business owner by relieving him or her of a great deal of stress caused by inadequate cash flow, but you often provide the cash for payroll which creates jobs and puts food on the tables of clients' employees. You are providing help to more people than you may even be aware.

17. Utilize my background, skills, and experiences.

Because you deal with both people and money, just about any kind of background will serve you well as a small factor. My own background as a pastor was tremendously helpful with the people end of the business; what I needed to learn was the business and money part, and while I was a slow learner at times, I found that part of it very enjoyable. Those who come from "people" professions may have a similar experience.

If you come from a business background, both the people and the money parts will be familiar to you because that's exactly what business is: people and money. If you believe business is nothing but money, you either haven't been in business before or you're not paying attention.

18. Provide ongoing challenges and not become another "boring job."

While procedures need to be followed, factoring is anything but boring. There are two reasons for this. 1) You're the boss and that automatically invests your heart and mind into what you're doing, especially where your money is involved. 2) No two clients or customers are alike, even in the same industry. Each business and business owner are unique, and exposure to them will provide a never-ending parade of interesting people and ventures right before your eyes. If you find this boring you need to take up extreme sports for a living.

19. Have training and/or support available.

The training you need to start as a small factor is found very inexpensively in the books which make up *The Small Factor Series* and other resources from Dash Point Publishing. The International Factoring Association (www.factoring.org) provides many workshops and other events throughout each year that are quite helpful. IFA also has a list of "preferred vendors" who sell products and services to specifically to factors.

20. Have minimal or no training costs.

The cost of *The Small Factor Series* is around $100. The Small Factor Academy is a complete online training system (www.SmallFactorAcademy.com) is less than $1000.

21. Have minimal or no ongoing support costs.

Unless you purchase a franchise, there are no royalty or other monthly payments due anyone. If you expect your software needs to go beyond spreadsheets, factoring software mentioned earlier will have subscription costs.

22. Require no special equipment, tools or machinery.

You very likely already have the office equipment you need: telephone and a computer or other device with an internet connection. E-fax services are inexpensive and there are a multitude from which to choose. If you need factoring software, that item will be one of your larger expenses. If you start with spreadsheets, however, this will not be an issue when you begin.

23. Require no inventory.

You stock nothing, manufacture nothing, sell no product, and have no raw materials to replenish. You provide a service with a universally needed commodity: cash. Because that's stored in your bank account, it doesn't take any room in your garage.

24. Require no particular clothing style (dress code, uniforms, etc.).

If you want to wear a tie at home I guess that's your business. Personally I prefer sweats and a T-shirt. Others sport their own "at-home clothes" at least a few hours a day. Just be sure you wear something appropriate when meeting a new client in person.

25. Allow the presence of my pet/s.

Maggie is my ever-faithful office assistant and constant companion throughout my work day. Her quite presence is calming to my soul and she is instantly ready to go if I need to drive somewhere. Unfortunately she's pretty useless answering the phone.

Clearly I'm a pet person, and having my devoted animal by my side all day every day provides great personal satisfaction in my work.

26. _____
Your comments:

27. _____
Your comments:

28. _____
Your comments:

29. _____
Your comments:

30. _____
Your comments:

Hopefully this chapter has helped you determine if factoring has the key characteristics you're looking for. If you've found that factoring small receivables does not meet your personal prerequisites, be glad you've learned that now before you've invested a dime of your money or another hour of your time. If it does meet your prerequisites, factoring can be a good fit for what you're seeking and wanting in an investment specifically, or for life in general.

11
Measuring Success & Determining What It Takes

How Do You Measure Success?

Success can be measured by a wide variety of yardsticks. We might divide the benchmarks for success into three broad categories:

1. Success measured by numbers
2. Success measured by client business advancement
3. Success measured by personal satisfaction

Success Measured by Numbers

Success is commonly gauged this way because it is easy to quantify. That is, you can tell if you are reaching specific goals because the numbers tell you. Success measured by numbers can include:

- The amount of gross income you generate.
- The amount of net income you generate.
- The amount of take home income you pay yourself.
- The amount of funds you have "on the street."
- The minimal amount of bad debt you absorb.
- The number of clients you have.
- The number of clients you retain.
- The number of staff you have.

Success Measured by Client Business Advancement

You may be inclined to measure your success by the benefit others derive from your efforts. If so, you are successful when you help people improve their businesses and their lives. You can measure this success by:

- The number of jobs you provide by enabling your clients to meet or increase payroll.
- The number of businesses you incubate with your service.
- The number of businesses you rejuvenate.
- The number of businesses you save from closing.

Success Measured by Personal Satisfaction

If you are choosing to invest in small receivables at least in part because of dissatisfaction with your present job or lifestyle, you likely will measure your success based on the personal satisfaction factoring can provide. While this is more subjective and thus harder to quantify, you'll consider yourself successful from:

- The personal satisfaction you feel being your own boss, making money independently, and helping a lot of other people.
- The realization that your work doesn't even feel like "work" because you enjoy what you do.
- The amount of free time you have to do the things you really want to do.
- The number of extra hugs your kids give you because you're home to receive them.

Pick any of the above yardsticks you'll use to measure your success, or come up with your own. Just have an idea of what *your* being a success is so that once you're under way, you know when you're reaching your goals and therefore succeeding. You'll also better understand what adjustments you need to make as you go so you will succeed.

What It Takes to Be Successful

Once you have a picture of what it will take for you to be a success in your own eyes, a healthy dose of self-examination is in order. Determining now if you have what it takes can relieve a lot of strain down the road, if you realize then you're not cut out for this type of activity.

Being a small factor requires certain skills, personal characteristics, and family support to manage the tasks well. Rest assured that you don't need to have all of these when you start; they can be learned or developed over time. Probably no one meets every single criterion, so don't feel you fall short if some of these don't describe you.

However having at least some of them when you begin will make the path to your success much easier. Consider each attribute below and identify a) those you already possess, and b) those you need to work on and develop.

Do You Have the Skills to Be a Small Factor?

People Skills

People skills refer to your ability to work with others. Consider these questions to determine the level of your own people skills:

- Do you like to work with others?
- Do others like to work with you?
- Do you enjoy talking with people in person and on the phone?
- Are you creative when it comes to solving a problem?
- Do you like to tackle problems and create solutions with others, or do you prefer to do these by yourself?
- Are you flexible yet level-headed?
- Do people trust you?
- Do people consider you to be fair?
- Do people say you are a good listener?
- Do you perceive what people's concerns, needs, and wants are from their words, gestures, or nonverbal clues?

- Are you discerning as to others' character and motives?
- Do people tend to take advantage of you?
- Are people ever afraid of you?

Business Skills

Identifying the level of your business skills will be easier if you've owned a business before. But whether you have or have not "been the boss," reflect on these aspects of your personality and background:

- Are you comfortable handling money?
- Is providing excellent value and service to customers/ clients important to you?
- Are you organized?
- How well do you manage your time?
- Do you understand and know how to interpret basic business financial reports like an income statement and balance sheet?
- Can you review a potential business transaction and know instinctively if it is a good or bad proposition?
- Do you make business purchases based on what is really needed or profitable for your company, or what you want personally?
- Can you make objective business decisions even when they affect a person or issue in which you have an emotional investment?
- Do you have contacts already established with others that will bring in potential new business?
- Do you have any marketing background that will help you obtain new clients?
- Do you recognize potential markets and know how to tap them?

Math/Computer Skills

While you need not be a college math major nor a nerdy computer geek, some basic skills will go a long way. Consider your response to the following issues:

- Higher math not included, do you enjoy arithmetic and working with numbers?
- Can you perform a simple calculation, look at the answer, and recognize immediately if the answer is way off? (For example, 25 x 100 = 250.)
- Do you grasp percentages and how to use them?
- Can you touch-type or do you "hunt & peck"?
- Do you enjoy entering data in a computer, including numbers?
- Do you have basic word processing, spreadsheet, data base, and internet skills?
- Do you enjoy learning new programs?

Do You Have the
Personal Characteristics Needed?

Tolerance for Risk

Like any investment factoring involves some element of risk. Therefore you need to be clear about your approach to and attitude about taking chances. Consider each of the following and the implications of your answers within the context of purchasing small receivables.

- Are you by nature a risk-taker or risk-avoider?
- Do you have a strong sense of fear or highly negative feelings at the thought of losing money from an investment?
- Do you get a "rush" from betting big in high stakes gambles?
- If you have lost money in previous investments, have you chosen to
  - Avoid such risk completely thereafter?
  - Continue in similar investments, learning to avoid making the same mistake again?
- Do you prefer to take some risks in order to receive a higher return, or do you prefer minimal risk with a lower return?

119

- Do you believe that taking no risk at all can pose a greater risk than taking a calculated risk?

Common Sense

As mentioned in the chapter "Risk and Its Management," common sense is your greatest ally. Be as objective as you can when considering these issues:

- Do people who know you well consider you to have common sense? (Ask them – an honest answer could surprise you!)
- Do you tend to make decisions based on impulse, emotion, or personal desires?
- When considering a new venture, do you tend to "dive in head first" or take a more methodical approach, scrutinizing all the angles before committing to a course of action?
- Can you postpone or suspend your personal desires for a perceived greater good?

Desire to Help

Altruism has its place when investing in receivables, though it must be tempered with common sense discussed above. Consider the following:

- Do you have a true desire in your heart to help others?
- Do you find satisfaction knowing that you have made the world a little better for at least one other person?
- Do others come to you when they need help?
- Do others consider you generous and compassionate?
- Do you give of your time and financial resources to charity or community service?

Trust Tempered with Caution

Ronald Reagan gave the famous directive "trust yet verify." Factoring the receivables of small business owners requires mutual trust yet also the need to keep one another honest.

- Do you usually believe everything people tell you?

- Do you have a basic trust in your fellow human, or do you believe that people are just looking out for themselves and will take advantage of you any chance they get?
- If you suspect someone is being dishonest with you, do you tend to dismiss your suspicions or assume your suspicions are correct?

Ability to Say "No"

There are times as a small factor when you will be faced with requests or opportunities. If you say "yes" to every single one you may become too busy, lose focus on what's important, or even lose money because of your decision. Consider your ability to say "no" in the following present or past circumstances:

- If you have children or grandchildren (of any age), are you able to say "no" to their requests when you think such an answer is best for them?
- Do you frequently agree to what others ask of you, only later to regret not declining their request?
- Do effective sales promotions often persuade you to buy a product even if you really don't need it?
- Do you politely listen to the full presentation of every telemarketer, even if you don't need or want what they're selling?
- Do you give to nearly all charities and worthy causes which ask you for a donation?

Do You Have the
Family Support You Need?

If you have absolutely no family – no spouse, significant other, children, parents, siblings, or anyone else from whom you derive love, support, acceptance, or self-worth – then the following section doesn't pertain to you.

However, many of you reading these pages very likely do have one or more such persons in your life, who is or are very important to you. Knowing how they feel about such a venture as factoring, how it may impact their lives, and the kind of support (or lack thereof) they give you can make a big difference. Think about the following issues as they pertain to the most important people in your life.

Financial Support

Whether you invest in receivables full-time or part-time, you might need additional income for at least some period of time. This may come from your regular job or the job of your spouse or the person providing financial resources for your household. Until you have enough capital and clients to be making enough to live on as a small factor, you will no doubt need continued financial support to meet living expenses.

If someone other than yourself is providing this financial support:

- Does he or she have a stable, permanent job or business they enjoy which will provide steady income for years to come?
- How long is he or she willing to continue in this role?
- Do you have a target date as to when your dependence on their income will cease?
- What is the chance of this person losing his/her source of income?
  - If that happens, what effect will it have on your factoring operation?

Moral Support

The person or persons closest to you probably have their own opinions about your factoring venture. Having the moral support of those important to you can have an effect on your attitude as well as your operation.

- Is this key person, or are these key people:
  - Working the business with you?
  - Just letting you "do your thing" and staying out of it?
  - Opposing what you're doing and wanting you to reject factoring?
- If they felt differently, what effect would that have on your desire to begin as a small factor?

Their Attitude Toward Risk

Each person has his or her own attitude toward risk. Within a family, and especially as a couple, two people might have very divergent points of view toward risk. At the two extremes, one might have a high degree of tolerance for risk, and the other may be completely risk averse. If this is true in your situation, the two of you need to have a heart-to-heart talk about this issue and come to an understanding before you enter too far into the factoring arena.

You may agree to disagree, but you do need to reach a mutual understanding on where you each stand and how that will impact your factoring practices. Especially if your spouse is the one who is risk averse and you are risk tolerant, agreeing on the risk management tools you will use (and then sticking to them once you're under way) can go a long way to alleviating anxiety of the risk averse person. Committing your risk management policy to writing and reviewing it periodically will help keep you on track.

+ + +

In closing this chapter, let me reinforce the fact that it's highly unlikely anyone meets every single desirable characteristic implied above. For that matter, few people will come to the table with many of these qualities. So understand that the more of these you possess and learn, the better you will perform, the higher your chance of success as you define it, and the more you will enjoy the tasks involved.

On the other hand, if you find you make absolutely no connections with any of what's been described and have no desire whatsoever to develop or learn them, then investing in small receivables is probably not for you. If that's the case, be glad you found this out now – before you invest your time and your or someone else's money, in something in which you probably would find neither enjoyment nor success!

12

Preparations

Decisions to Make

Having determined that factoring meets your desires and having carefully considered the success and personality issues from the previous chapter, we now turn to the task of making preliminary preparations.

Committing these preparations to writing in one form or another can be very helpful. Some will want to spend the time on a business plan and/or marketing plan. Especially if you intend to begin factoring full-time immediately, this is not a bad idea. For those who intend to enter part-time, it's a good idea to jot down your general ideas and direction but a full-blown business plan might be more than necessary.

In either case, you will need to think about each of the following and make notes as to what you intend to do. These will involve deciding upon or choosing:

1. A few trusted advisors to whom you can turn for advice and counsel. These can include:
   - a business attorney
   - an accountant
   - a friend or relative with good business acumen
   - an experienced factor.

2. Your participation in factoring as a part-time private investment, or part-time or full-time business.

   If you decide to do this as a business you'll need to select the type of business under which you'll operate. You can be a:
   - Sole Proprietor

- Corporation
- Limited Liability Corporation, or
- Partnership.

A corporation or LLC probably hold the most advantages, but you should consult your attorney and accountant before making a final decision.

3. The geographical market and specific industries you'll target for clients.

4. The marketing methods you will use.

5. The logistical needs you will have including:
    - Office and supplies
    - Documents and forms
    - Web site
    - Software

6. A timeline for your marketing tasks and logistical needs. Sketch these on paper to focus and direct your actions and stay on schedule.

7. The finances you'll use to start. If more are needed later, the methods you will use to secure them.

8. A working budget.

9. Specific risk management practices you will follow.

Below is a sample budget to get you started. You may wish to add and/or rename some categories below. Keep in mind a budget is a plan to guide you on your way; it's normal to make adjustments as your operation continues and matures.

Sample Budget

<u>Monthly Income</u>

Factoring Discounts	$_____
Commissions from Brokered Clients	$_____
Administrative Fees	$_____
Interest Earned	$_____
Other Income	$_____
Total Income	$_____

<u>Monthly Expenses</u>

Office Rent	$_____
Office Utilities	$_____
Office Telephone	$_____
Fax	$_____
Cell phone	$_____
Computer Expenses	$_____
Internet connection	$_____
Web site	$_____
Factoring Software	$_____
Cost of Capital (Loan interest)	$_____
Broker/Finder Fees	$_____
Office Supplies	$_____
Due Diligence expenses	$_____
Marketing	$_____
Legal	$_____
Accountant	$_____
Taxes	$_____
Payroll/Salary	$_____
Bad Debt Reserve	$_____
Other	$_____
Total Expenses	$_____
Net Profit	$_____

Sample Policy for
Minimization of Risk

Dash Point Financial Services, Inc.

We utilize the following policies to minimize risk and preserve capital.

Financial Limits

1. We usually invest no more than 10% of our pool of capital into any client or customer.

2. Because a factor's greatest risk is often at the beginning of a new account, we prefer clients start with around $5,000 in factored receivables, and accept only clients who begin factoring $10,000 a month or less.

3. We put a credit limit of $10,000 on each new account and do not provide access to more funds until a client has proven to be honest, to be running a well-managed operation, and has customers who pay in a timely and/or relatively predictable manner.

4. When credit limits are raised above the initial $10,000, it is usually done in increments of $5,000.

5. Once a client reaches $60,000 in steady monthly volume, we refer them to a larger factor and no longer work with them, limiting our exposure with any one client to this amount. This could also provide the client with access to slightly better discount rates larger factors may provide, while enabling us to maintain our rates for new small clients and often receive a broker commission from the larger factor. Alternately, we may participate with another factor in funding this client. Either practice limits our exposure.

6. We do not purchase individual invoices larger than $15,000. Our preferred invoice size is $200 to $5,000, and we charge a $10 minimum invoice discount to avoid very small invoices.

Among all our clients, the average invoice size we purchase is approximately $2500.

7. We limit the amount of invoices factored to a specific customer (i.e. the company paying the invoice) to $50,000. This limits our exposure to one customer who might be shared by more than one client.

Reserve Accounts

1. We set aside 10% off the top of all discounts into an interest bearing Bad Debt Reserves account and access this account only in the event of a loss.

2. With new clients we establish an escrow reserve account that is accumulated from a small deduction from advances given. This reserve is built up to and maintained at a level of 10% of their credit limit.

Due Diligence

1. We run credit reports on prospects' and clients' customers prior to purchasing invoices they will be paying. If credit history is not found, clients provide an aging report showing the customer's payment history. If this is not available, such customers are usually declined.

2. We run a public record check on prospective clients prior to approving them to determine if any judgments, liens, or bankruptcies have been filed. Criminal background checks are run as well.

3. Each invoice is sent with our post office box as the remit to address. This lessens the possibility of misdirection of customer payments. Our bank lockbox automatically deposits customer checks into our bank account, regardless of the company name to whom the checks are made.

4. We obtain a signed Notice of Assignment from a customer before advancing initial funds for that customer's invoices.

5. We regularly monitor aging reports and flagged invoices of current outstanding receivables to become aware of slow and late payers. Follow up calls are made in a professional manner which keep unnecessarily slow payments and non-payments to a minimum.

6. We regularly track client and customer concentrations using graphs provided in our software. The average concentration per client is about 3%, and per customer is about .5%, keeping our exposures very low throughout the portfolio.

7. We factor solely on a recourse basis. That is, if an invoice is not paid by the customer for any reason, the client must replace it with a new one, and/or repay the advance plus discount from their escrow reserve account and/or future advances and/or rebates.

8. We require personal guarantees from each new client.

9. We file UCC1 forms on each new client. This places a lien on their assets, protecting our investment from garnishment from vendors and places us in first position in the case of a client bankruptcy.

10. We file an 8821 Form with IRS for each new client. This instructs IRS to notify us if there is impending action being taken against the client for unpaid income or payroll taxes. Thus we can work out an arrangement on behalf of the client to meet negotiated IRS obligations from regular advances, while keeping our investment in the client secure. This is rarely needed, however.

General Provisions
1. We do not purchase invoices for services or products that have not yet been delivered.

2. We do not provide private or business loans to clients. Funds are advanced only on factored invoices.

3. We do not purchase the following:
   - Consumer receivables, which have a high rate of default and then are often difficult to collect.
   - Construction receivables, a specialized factoring field.
   - Medical receivables covered by third party insurance companies, Medicare, Medicaid, or private patient payments. Such receivables are quite complicated, pay very inconsistently, and require extensive back office needs. We do welcome medical receivables which are paid by hospitals and other businesses with good credit ratings and involve ordinary factoring procedures.
   - Transportation receivables, due to the higher risk of late payment or nonpayment because of improperly submitted paperwork.
   - International receivables, which require specialized expertise.
   - Purchase Orders for non-government receivables.

4. We limit the number of clients in our portfolio so we can efficiently manage them and provide excellent client service.

13
Four Sample Small Factors

Now that we've laid the foundations for becoming a small factor, let's look at the lives of a few people who have made the decision to invest in small receivables. As you will see, each is different in age, marital status, background and experiences, motivation, personal goals, and perspectives on success. However, each has found factoring to be a good fit for his or her circumstances.

While your situation is unique, you may identify with certain aspects of one or more of these individuals. Their circumstances and decisions may help clarify your own.

Gene and Linda

Gene is the individual referred to in the chapter "Is This Right for You?" He is 30 years old and has worked in the telecommunications industry since graduating from college. He has found after eight years that the corporate world is not where he wants to spend the next 35 years of his life.

Because of this realization he has carefully and methodically researched scores of potential business and investment opportunities to find the one that fits his needs. You may recall his three requirements are that the business 1) have little or no upfront capital expenditures, 2) be an enterprise he can work from home, and 3) enable him to begin part-time and allow him to ease into full-time.

His fiancée, Linda, is 33 and has recently completed medical school. She works in a specialized field with steady demand for her expertise. She and Gene wish to begin a family fairly soon after their upcoming marriage, and both want to be home as much as possible once their children are born.

Since finishing college Gene has managed to set aside about $50,000 from his work, which he plans to use as seed capital to begin factoring part-time. He calculates that within about six months' time, assuming most of this is invested in receivables, turns consistently, and he experiences no significant bad debt, this capital pool will provide approximately $2,000 in monthly income for his part-time factoring business.

Because they still have Linda's medical school debts to pay, they will have regular monthly obligations to meet in addition to normal living expenses. Once these debts are retired Gene and Linda plan to invest into his factoring company the same amount they had been paying for the school bills. This will provide additional working capital to fund his expanding client base.

They estimate that within 18 months these funds and the extra income they generate will enable Gene to leave his present job and devote full-time to his factoring business. At that time Linda will work part-time because she wants to be at home with her children, but still maintain her medical practice on a somewhat limited basis. Doing so will provide dependable income for their family.

Gene has obtained an attorney and accountant from referrals made by on-site professional colleagues at his present company. Gene's experience in his industry has given him an excellent preparation in the business world, and he has established a friendship with a factor he found on the internet who has agreed to provide him answers to procedural questions he might have as his business develops. In exchange for this advice, he has agreed to refer larger deals he finds through his marketing efforts to this factor – deals which are larger than the clients he is targeting.

Gene will be marketing to janitorial companies and temp agencies in the greater Boston area where he lives, seeking those with annual gross income volumes less than $500,000. He will be seeking firms who wish to factor $5,000 in receivables to start, with minimum invoices of $100 in size. He has set a starting credit limit of $10,000 per client, and will not continue to fully fund clients when their monthly volume exceeds $20,000. When that happens he will seek to participate with a larger factor who will allow him to continue to advance his limited funds for that client with the partnering factor.

He will start marketing with a direct mail campaign using postcards and a mailing list he obtained from a marketing list provider he found on the internet. He will send out 100-200 cards on a weekly basis and is hoping for a 2% return, which would result in two to four inquiries per week – about what he can manage while he keeps his present full-time job.

Gene has maintained a home office for the past few years, as he occasionally works in the evenings and on weekends from home. He has a computer and tablet and plans to order a distinctive ring service from his telephone company which will piggyback onto his current line. The distinctive ring number will be his business number while he works as a part-time factor. Once he goes full time, he will order a separate line and switch his business number to that line. He also has an account with an e-fax service which provides a fax number with which he can receive faxes via email.

Having knowledge of web site development Gene has created his own site for marketing and making his application documents available online. He is using the documents described and utilized in the book *Factoring Small Receivables* (book 2 in this series), after giving them to his lawyer to review and adapt to his operation.

Gene plans to utilize spreadsheets to track his factoring activity until he has four clients, then upgrade to a commercial factoring software package. He currently uses Quicken for his personal bookkeeping, and will upgrade to QuickBooks or Xero which will track his business accounting as his new business starts.

Gene's measure of success is to be factoring full-time in 18 months and earning an average of $4,000 per month by that time. Another benchmark will be to increase his factoring income a minimum of 25% each year for three years. He will also be successful when the time he spends sharing parental responsibilities is equal to Linda's.

Donna

Donna is a 45-year-old mother of two who divorced three years ago. Her children are in high school and live with her. After working in management for two different corporations, then for the county government in its purchasing department, Donna was downsized due to budget cuts and has been unemployed for four months. Her unemployment benefits will end in two months and when that happens she will need to earn enough income to meet her household expenses.

During her work for the county she observed a few vendors having their payments directed to a post office box or other location different from their business address. She didn't think much about this until she learned about factoring. Since the county paid with 45 day terms, this service was a great benefit to these vendors who provided lawn service, vehicle maintenance, and potentially thousands of other goods and services. The county's vendor list was extensive.

Donna's personal requirements for her factoring venture are that she:

- Work at home and be present when her kids arrive home from school.
- Earn a living income within twelve months after starting
- Have minimal expenses to start.
- Utilize her skills and extensive contacts from her previous work experience.

She expects factoring small receivables will meet these requirements.

Donna has realized that with the portion of money she set aside in retirement funds, she can begin buying a few small clients' receivables and at the same time broker larger factoring accounts and three other cash flow instruments she learned in the course. She estimates that in about a year's time the combined income from these efforts will replace the monthly paycheck she had been earning, and certainly be larger than the unemployment checks she has learned to live on.

She has an acquaintance in the District Attorney's office who referred her to a business attorney in her town, who in turn referred her to an accountant. Her sister lives across town, has owned various successful businesses over the years, and is quite willing to act as a sounding board for any business questions Donna might have.

She expects to find at least a couple very small factoring clients which most of the larger factors will not want, so she intends to fund them herself with a 401 (k) account she has saved, plus funds borrowed from her sister, to whom she will pay 12% simple interest. She has completed the paperwork to begin her service as a Sole Proprietor, and when she begins purchasing accounts she will incorporate her business.

Because of her close contacts with the county purchasing department, Donna plans to focus on marketing to vendors of the county. As this is such an extensive list, and she also has contacts with city and state purchasing departments, she will have a virtually limitless marketing list to prospect. She plans to target approximately 100 businesses per week and make telephone calls to the owners to see if any of her cash flow streams can help them. Her goal will be to call 20 such businesses each day.

She has a desk in the corner of her bedroom which will serve as her office. Her home computer will double as the office computer, and she'll add a distinctive ring service for her business calls. She has set up an email account for her business with one of the free providers, and is using an online website creation service to develop her own web site.

Once she begins factoring her own clients, she'll start with spreadsheets to track them. If she doesn't fund more than three or four clients, as she expects, this will probably be adequate for her needs. Since she has used an online bookkeeping program to track her personal expenses and is comfortable with this program, she plans to use it for her business as well.

Donna's long-term definition of success will be to provide a steady $6,000 per month in take-home income. Meanwhile, she has set incremental steps of increasing her income by 20% quarterly until she reaches the $6,000 monthly goal.

Carl, Sharon, and Cindy

Carl is 56 and has been the owner of a family-run radiator shop for over thirty years. Simply put, he is ready to do something new. The grind of long days and keeping employees on task has taken its toll, and he is ready for clean work he can do from home with his wife, Sharon, and grown daughter, Cindy. Both have an interest in working with him in the factoring business.

Carl has chosen factoring because he wants to work from home, put in shorter days than the shop required, and be free on weekends. He also wants to have time to play tennis a couple times each week. He wants a business that will utilize his skills and those of Sharon and Cindy, so that the learning curve for each is relatively short.

Because Carl has many contacts in the business community and his wife and daughter have handled the office tasks over the years, Carl's main job will be using his networking contacts to bring in business and his business experience to approve accounts. Sharon and Cindy will share the data entry, bookkeeping, record keeping, and due diligence tasks.

Much of Carl's radiator service involved work on the fleets of delivery trucks for local businesses. He factored some of these receivables over the last several years and knows first-hand what a boost the improved cash flow can provide a small business. He also recognizes that acting as a factor himself can be an enjoyable and profitable business, without many of the headaches and long, tiring days to which he is accustomed.

He has known and used an attorney from his church for quite some time, and his radiator shop accountant is willing to continue as he starts his new venture. His many years of running a successful shop have seasoned Carl well for his new factoring business. He remains on good terms with the factor with whom he's worked, who has consented to answer factoring questions he may have from time to time.

Carl sold his radiator business for a good price and intends to use the proceeds from the sale, plus some savings he's accumulated over the years, to finance his factoring operation. He is also on good terms with his banker who knows his good business sense. While he intends to start slowly, he plans to become full-time as soon as is feasible. Upon the advice of his attorney, he has created a new LLC with himself, Sharon and Cindy as members.

He will begin marketing to the lengthy list of customers from his shop and already knows those who have had cash flow problems of their own. The new owner is happy to allow Carl to use this list, because the business customers who factor with Carl will have improved cash flow and be able to pay the new radiator shop owner in a timely fashion.

Being a long-time member of the Chamber of Commerce and Lions Club, his contacts are extensive and he is confident they will produce an ongoing list of referrals. He's made it known to friends and associates that he'll be happy to provide finders fees for leads which turn into business, and this has piqued the interest of these long-time acquaintances.

When Carl sold his business the office was part of the sale. However, purchasing a couple computers, office furniture, and telephones are a quite minor expense for his circumstances. The large bonus room in his house – little used since his kids left home – will serve as the office, and provide space for growth as needed.

Carl kept all the factoring documents he signed when he first factored, and asked the factor if there were any other documents he should use. He then had his attorney review these documents. His son-in-law works with computers and is happy to create a web site for the business, Carl plans to use a professional factoring data base program right from the start. Sharon has used QuickBooks for years in the radiator business, and intends to use it to track their bookkeeping records now.

Carl's measure of success will come in the personal satisfaction of working six-hour days from home, and having no employees other than his family. With the funds at his disposal, he anticipates a monthly income before expenses of $10,000, and will consider a bad debt loss of 2% annually to be a mark of success.

In short, Carl is well-positioned to begin as a new factor. He has years of business experience, adequate funds to work full-time, an experienced staff in his family, excellent community contacts, and a long-standing network for new and continuing business.

Frank

Frank is a man of 67 who retired a few years ago after a successful career as an accountant. Though his wife's health has been gradually declining over the last year, Frank enjoys good health and is quite physically active. He wants an investment that will allow him to be available for his wife, leave him time for the two rounds of golf he enjoys with his buddies each week, and make good use of his professional skills and the expertise he's developed over the years. Naturally, he's looking for an investment that will provide an excellent return.

Frank has known about factoring for some time from his years as a CPA. He incorporated his own part-time consulting business a few years before he retired, and providing factoring services is a very natural extension of other financial services he offers.

He has had long-standing business relationships with attorneys, is a seasoned business professional, and has made contact with some local larger factors over the course of his career. If he needs their expertise, they are happy to provide it.

Frank intends to factor on a part-time basis for the next several years. He has plenty of contacts with business owners who will provide him leads. These contacts come from his current consulting, his former CPA firm, and his years of being a part of the community. Just as word of mouth has kept him busy as a financial consultant, he expects it will do the same for his factoring practice.

His home office has been in place for some time. He will add some pages describing his factoring service to his already existing web site, and he intends to use commercial factoring data base software because he doesn't want to spend unnecessary time tending to spreadsheets. He is quite familiar with a variety of accounting programs, any of which will meet his business needs.

Frank will measure his success by the time he spends with his wife, maintaining his golf time, and the number of factoring clients whose businesses he will incubate, grow, and/or resurrect. He is confident of his success using these benchmarks, and looks forward to the benefits he and his clients will enjoy.

As you can see, factoring is a natural fit for Frank's circumstances. He will continue to use his knowledge and expertise, has a built-in referral base, can take on as many clients as he chooses and then no more to maintain his free time, and he will make an excellent return on investment.

+ + +

While these four examples are unique and come to factoring from very different positions in life, investing in receivables meets the specific requirements of each quite nicely.

Gene and Linda, fairly early in their careers and life together, want a business with low start up expenses which can be done from home starting part-time. At a slow but steady pace it will grow to become a lucrative business for them, providing handsomely for their soon to be growing family.

Donna needs something that will allow her to start her life anew after some difficult times, and keep her at home to maintain her relationships with her kids. In time her business will provide excellent income for herself and her family.

Carl and Sharon are looking for a change of pace from the work they've known for three decades, yet want to make use of the skills and contacts they've developed over that time. They see factoring as a great family business for themselves and their grown daughter, Cindy, who one day will inherit and run the business when Carl and Sharon retire. They have adequate capital to earn enough discounts for a full-time income, and they can grow the business as large as they desire.

Frank is also looking forward to keeping his business skills sharp. But even more, he's ready to have the time with his wife that he needs, the time for golf that he wants, and an excellent return on a hands-on investment that he enjoys. The good that his factoring service will provide for his clients and their employees is icing on the cake.

Conclusion

As you can see, factoring can meet the financial and personal goals of many different people coming from a broad array of backgrounds, education, and life circumstances. While factoring is not a perfect fit for every person, it is an excellent means of meeting the needs of many people.

I urge you to take the time to determine exactly what you are seeking in your own life, what specific needs you have, and consider whether factoring small receivables can meet those needs, as it did for the four households described in the last chapter.

If you find that factoring is not the right match for your circumstances just now or for your life in general, then I'm glad you've determined this without the investment of significant time or money. If it is right for you, you are in for an interesting and potentially profitable venture, and I wish you all the best. I sincerely hope this book and those that follow in this series provide you with helpful and instructive direction as you learn more about becoming a small factor.

Whatever your circumstances, best wishes to you in your endeavors!

Appendix

Books and Ebooks by Jeff Callender

The Small Factor Series

Book 1
Factoring Wisdom:
A Preview of
Buying Receivables

Short Sayings and Straight Talk
For New & Small Factors

Book 2
Fundamentals
for Factors

How You Can Make
Large Returns in Small Receivables

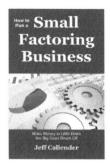

Book 3
How to Run
a Small Factoring Business

Make Money in Little Deals
the Big Guys Brush Off

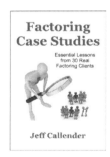

Book 4
***Factoring Case Studies
(2nd Edition)***

Essential Lessons from
30 Real Factoring Clients

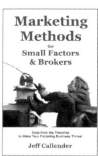

Book 5
***Marketing Methods
for Small Factors
and Brokers***

Tools from the Trenches
To Make Your Factoring Business Thrive!

About This Series

The Small Factor Series is designed to:

1. Provide a succinct introduction and summary of the books in this series as well as other writings by Jeff Callender.

2. Introduce readers to the investment of factoring small business receivables.

3. Provide a step-by-step manual with complete instructions for small factors.

4. Provide 30 real-life examples of factoring clients from the files of people who have been investing in small receivables for some time.

5. Describe and analyze numerous marketing methods to bring in new business which have been used by the eight contributors to the book.

Each book in the series is written to address the above points:

- Book 1, *Factoring Wisdom: A Preview of Buying Receivables,* introduces and summarizes the other books with brief excerpts from each, and arranges them by subject matter.

- Book 2, *Fundamentals for Factors* introduces potential factors to the business.

- Book 3, *How to Run a Small Factoring Business,* is the step-by-step manual.

- Book 4, *Factoring Case Studies* (2nd Edition), describes experiences of 30 real clients of small factors, which illustrate the many lessons and suggestions made in Books 2 and 3.

- Book 5, *Marketing Methods for Small Factors & Brokers,* includes contributions from seven small factors and an experienced broker.

Other Books by Jeff Callender

Factoring: Sell Your Invoices Today, Get Cash Tomorrow

How to Obtain Unlimited Funds without a Loan

Written to introduce factoring to small business owners, this book compares factoring to traditional lending, shows how it can help a company's cash flow, and guides readers in determining if factoring can improve their business.

The above books are available in the following formats from DashPointPublishing.com:

- Paperback
- PDF
- Kindle
- iPad & Android

Ebooks by Jeff Callender

Accounting Methods for Factors and Their Clients

By Robert Vasquez and Jeff Callender

This ebook describes how to establish and maintain proper bookkeeping records for a factoring company and factoring clients. You'll learn how to use GAAP-approved procedures and make sure you're doing it right. Following these step-by-step instructions starts you on the right foot.

How I Run My One-Person Factoring Business

Want to get started running a small factoring business by yourself? This ebook shows how the author successfully began as a one-person operation, and the everyday tools you can use now to do the same.

How I Run My Virtual Factoring Office

A virtual office means you can work from just about anywhere you want. Learn the common tools and technology the author uses (available to anyone) to run his virtual factoring office. Enjoy the comforts of home – at work!

"Top 10" Ebooks by Jeff Callender

"Top 10" Ebooks for Factors:

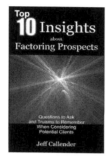

Top 10 Insights
about Factoring Prospects

Questions to Ask
and Truisms to Remember
When Considering Potential Clients

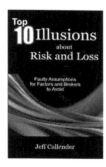

Top 10 Illusions
about Risk and Loss

Faulty Assumptions for
Factors and Brokers to Avoid

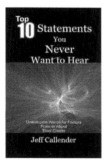

Top 10 Statements
You Never Want to Hear

Unwelcome Words for Factors
From or About Their Clients

10 Key Points to Look for in Factoring Software

Consider these 10 issues *before* purchasing software for your factoring operation

"Top 10" Ebooks for Clients:

Top 10 Quotes on the Benefits of Factoring

Statements from Business Owners Who Factor Their Receivables

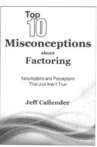

Top 10 Misconceptions about Factoring

Assumptions and Perceptions That Just Aren't True

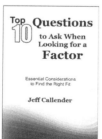

Top 10 Questions to Ask When Looking for a Factor

Essential Considerations to Find the Right Fit

The above ebooks are available in the following formats from DashPointPublishing.com:

- PDF
- Kindle
- iPad & Android (ePub)

Acknowledgments

I would like to thank the following people for their important contributions to this book:

Nicole Jones for her proofreading skills and creating the ebook versions of books in the *Small Factor Series* and all other titles, and making them available to the world.

Anne Gordon for her proofreading skills and valuable experience, comments, suggestions, and support.

The new and aspiring small factors who asked numerous questions which led to the creation of this book.

Important Notice

This publication is for educational purposes only and is not intended to give legal, tax, or professional advice. If such service is needed, the reader should seek professional advice from a competent attorney or accountant.

The author and publisher assume no responsibility for any financial losses a reader may experience as a result of any factoring or other business or investment transaction.

Also by Jeff Callender

Paperbacks and Ebooks
The Small Factor Series includes 5 titles:

1. *Factoring Wisdom: A Preview of Buying Receivables*
   Short Sayings and Straight Talk for New & Small Factors   © 2012

2. *Fundamentals for Factors*
   How You Can Make Large Returns in Small Receivables   © 2012

3. *How to Run a Small Factoring Business*
   Make Money in Little Deals the Big Guys Brush Off   © 2012

4. *Factoring Case Studies*
   Essential Lessons from 30 Real Factoring Clients
                    1st edition ©2003, 2005; 2nd edition © 2012

5. *Marketing Methods for Small Factors & Brokers*
   Tools from the Trenches to Make Your Factoring Business Thrive!
                                                      © 2012

Factoring: Sell Your Invoices Today & Get Cash Tomorrow
   How to Obtain Unlimited Funds without a Loan   © 2012

eBooks
For Factoring Clients:

Accounting Methods for Factors & Their Clients   © 2012
Top 10 Quotes on the Benefits of Factoring   © 2012
Top 10 Misconceptions about Factoring   © 2012
Top 10 Questions to Ask When Looking for a Factor   © 2012

For Factors:

Accounting Methods for Factors & Their Clients   © 2012
How I Run My One-Person Factoring Business   © 2008, 2012
How I Run My Virtual Factoring Office   © 2012
Top 10 Insights about Factoring Prospects   © 2008, 2012
Top 10 Illusions about Risk and Loss   © 2008, 2012
Top 10 Statements You Never Want to Hear   © 2008, 2012
10 Key Points to Look for in Factoring Software   © 2008, 2012

Spreadsheet Calculators
APR and Income Calculators   © 2002, 2012

Software
FactorFox Software   © 2006 – current year

Websites
www.DashPointPublishing.com   www.SmallFactor.com
www.DashPointFinancial.com   www.SmallFactorAcademy.com
www.FactorFox.com   www.FactorFind.com

About the Author

Jeff Callender had an unusual start to his business career. Though he is the son and grandson of businessmen, he began his working life as a pastor.

After earning a college degree in Sociology and a Master of Divinity degree, he served three churches in Washington state over 14 years. While he found ministry rewarding, he realized he had an entrepreneurial spirit which gradually pulled him toward business.

He left his career in the church and about a year later stumbled onto factoring. He began as a broker but after numerous referrals were declined only because of their small size, he started factoring very small clients himself. His career as a factor – and as a pioneer in the niche of very small receivables factoring – was thus born in 1994.

He has worked with a great number of very small business owners in need of factoring. He wrote his first book, *Factoring Small Receivables*, in 1995, and since then has written numerous books, ebooks, and articles, and spoken at many events in the factoring industry. His writing and two decades of experience have established him as a leading authority in the niche of small business factoring.

Jeff is the President of three companies he started. Dash Point Financial provides factoring services to small business owners throughout the U.S. It also provides the nucleus of his experience for writing. Learn more at DashPointFinancial.com.

Dash Point Publishing publishes and sells his books and ebooks, as well as those of other authors who write about factoring. His paperbacks are available from DashPointPublishing.com, as well as Amazon, the Kindle bookstore, Apple's iBookstore, and other online ebook sellers. Dash Point Publishing's website provides additional materials such as legal documents for smaller factoring companies.

FactorFox Software offers a cloud-based database solution for factors to track their client transactions. Originally based on his own company's back-office operational needs, readers of his books will feel right at home using the software in their own factoring companies. It has become one of the top platforms for the industry and is used by factoring companies throughout the world. More information can be found at FactorFox.com.

Having grown up in southern California, Jeff now lives in Tacoma, Washington with his wife, dog, and two cats. He has a grown son and daughter.

Made in the
USA
Columbia, SC